The Ecumenical Work of the Icon

The Ecumenical Work of the Icon

Bringing the Iconographic Tradition
to Catholic Seminaries

HILDA KLEIMAN

WIPF & STOCK · Eugene, Oregon

THE ECUMENICAL WORK OF THE ICON
Bringing the Iconographic Tradition to Catholic Seminaries

Copyright © 2018 Hilda Kleiman. All rights reserved. Except for brief quotations in critical publications or reviews, no part of this book may be reproduced in any manner without prior written permission from the publisher. Write: Permissions, Wipf and Stock Publishers, 199 W. 8th Ave., Suite 3, Eugene, OR 97401.

Wipf & Stock
An Imprint of Wipf and Stock Publishers
199 W. 8th Ave., Suite 3
Eugene, OR 97401

www.wipfandstock.com

PAPERBACK ISBN: 978-1-5326-1650-1
HARDCOVER ISBN: 978-1-4982-4034-5
EBOOK ISBN: 978-1-4982-4033-8

Revised Standard Version Bible, Ignatius Edition, copyright 2006 by the Division of Christian Education of the National Council of the Churches of Christ in the United States of America. Used by permission. All rights reserved.

Manufactured in the U.S.A.

For my students, past and present, and for all of my colleagues within the Iconographic Arts Institute. May God be glorified!

And the Word became flesh and dwelt among us, full of grace and truth; we have beheld his glory, glory as of the only-begotten Son of the Father.

JOHN 1:14

Just as we have borne the image of the man of dust, we shall also bear the image of the man of heaven.

1 CORINTHIANS 15:49

Contents

List of Illustrations | viii
Preface | ix
Acknowledgments | xi
Introduction | xiii

1 Joining the Conversation: The Ecumenical Movement | 1
    Documents of the Second Vatican Council   1
    Directory for the Application of Principles and Norms of Ecumenism   12
    Ut Unum Sint: On Commitment to Ecumenism and Additional Contributions   16
    Receptive Ecumenism and Catholic Learning   26
    Orthodoxy and Ecumenism   41

2 Contributing to the Conversation: The Iconographic Tradition | 55
    The Theology of the Icon   57
    The Vocation of the Iconographer   60
    The Icon and the Liturgy   64
    The Iconographic Canon   70
    The Iconoclast Controversy   81
    Treatise III of *On the Divine Images*: A Summary and Response   91
    The Icon in Twentieth-Century Russia   96

3 Inviting Others into the Conversation: Application | 105
    The Iconographic Arts Institute   105
    Mount Angel Seminary   117
    The Iconographic Tradition beyond Catholic Seminaries   131

Bibliography | 135

Illustrations

Icon of the Holy Face | 108

Icon of the Mother of God | 112

Icon of Saint Matthew | 120

Icon of the Pantocrator | 123

Preface
The Studious Believer

WHEN I BEGAN THEOLOGICAL studies at Mount Angel Seminary in 2006, I was introduced to a definition of a theologian that has continued to resonate with me as I have been drawn into new areas of theology through my studies and teaching. In his book *The Shape of Catholic Theology*, Aidan Nichols explains that a student is a theologian when he or she takes his or her studies as "a solemn engagement to developing over a lifetime the gift of Christian wonder, of curiosity."[1] The theologian, he explains, is the studious believer who asks "why?" As the completion of my MA at Mount Angel Seminary coincided with the beginning of my more formal study of iconography, I started asking why about iconography and Orthodox Christianity and how to approach them as a Catholic, as a student of the icon, and as a member of the faculty of a Catholic seminary.

While I had the benefit of my theological studies at Mount Angel Seminary when I began studying iconography through the Iconographic Arts Institute in 2009, I was, in some respects, starting with very little background. For five years prior to the official start of my study of iconography, I observed the institute students and teachers by visiting their studio as much as I could during the weeklong institute each summer, but due to other responsibilities, I was not able to observe their process in its entirety. Before 2009, I had not dedicated much time to reading on iconography or Orthodoxy, and I had only made a few brief visits to an Orthodox church. The first of those visits occurred when I was a freshman in college and my philosophy professor took a group of his students to Saint Nicholas

---

1. Nichols, *Shape of Catholic Theology*, 19.

Orthodox Church in Portland, Oregon, for Vespers. The sheer number of icons and amount of incense in the church was splendid, yet at the time I did not follow up on that experience with additional questions for my professor or reading on my own.

Since 2009, I have been learning as much about iconography and the Orthodox tradition as I can through the institute, individual reading and study, receiving lessons from a master iconographer, and visiting Orthodox churches whenever possible. Sometimes my reading about the Orthodox tradition speaks of those who are learning about the Orthodox Church, regardless of whether they have the explicit intention of becoming Orthodox themselves, as being on a journey to Orthodoxy. Even as a Catholic, I find this an appropriate way of describing the process in which I have been engaged with the icon and the work that continues to grow from it. I am on my own journey to Orthodoxy, which is a part of a journey toward greater Christian unity as well. I understand this book as a description and significant part of that journey.

In some respects I am hesitant to speak about that journey, in part because of my relatively limited experience with Orthodoxy thus far. However, I still find myself being remade in how I see and experience the Christian faith. Simply put, there was life before I was introduced to iconography and Orthodoxy, and there is life after I was introduced to iconography and Orthodoxy. This book specifically offers my colleagues and students, many of whom have also had a limited exposure to Orthodoxy and iconography, what I have learned during this journey thus far.

At times this is an uneasy journey, and I expect it will continue to be so. I have encountered the Christian faith in ways that I had not experienced before I began training as an iconographer. I have experienced a call to think, speak, and act in new ways, to further conversion, to *theosis*. I think this uneasiness and apprehension is as it should be. Faithfulness to the study of iconography means that conversion must be a real possibility. I have experienced the Lord through this study, and my hope is that through this study my colleagues, students, and members of the wider Christian community will draw closer to him as well.

Acknowledgments

My gratitude to my teachers at the Iconographic Arts Institute, Claudia Coose, Mary Katsilometes, and Kathy Sievers, especially for their support as I have found my place in the spectrum of callings to iconography.

I would also like to thank my colleagues at Mount Angel Seminary, particularly Dr. Owen F. Cummings, for his encouragement of an earlier version of this project, and Dr. Shawn Keough and Dr. Jodi Kilcup, for their readings of an earlier version of this project. I am also grateful to Dr. Mark Nussberger for his interest in the icon and his moral support during the final stages of writing this book.

Introduction

The Ecumenical Work of the Icon

A SIGNIFICANT PORTION OF the training undertaken by Kathy Sievers and Mary Katsilometes, master iconographers and two of the instructors for the Iconographic Arts Institute, was with Father Egon Sendler, a Jesuit priest who did much work toward the recovery of the iconographic tradition in the twentieth century. That tradition has been and continues to be rediscovered not only by the Orthodox but by Catholics and many Protestant denominations as well. At one point in her time with Father Sendler, Mary Katsilometes asked him what he thought was happening through the recovery of the iconographic tradition in the West. What was the reason for it? Why was it happening now? Father Sendler replied that while he did not fully understand what was happening, he was sure of two parts of this dynamic: the recovery of the iconographic tradition is the work of the Holy Spirit, and it is ecumenical. The renewed interest in iconography has a place within God's work of salvation.[1] This insight is so central to the work of the institute that Fr. Sendler's statement heads the introduction to the booklet that contains the curriculum for the Certificate in Iconographic Arts, which the institute inaugurated in 2016.

Mary has shared the story of her conversation with Father Sendler with her students many times, and it always left me wondering what it means to say that the icon is ecumenical. As my own studies have progressed, I have gathered more questions that build on that initial one. What does it mean for Catholics and other Christians, as well as for the Orthodox, to say that the icon is ecumenical? How does our answer to this question shape how

1. Mary Katsilometes (master iconographer), in discussion with the author, November 2012.

and why we approach icons, both in prayer and as iconographers and students of the icon? What do I need to know and need to be able to share with others in order to understand the icon as ecumenical and to participate in its ecumenical work?

In this book, I claim that as Catholic Christian iconographers and students of the icon, our best approach to iconography includes understanding and joining the conversation that is the ecumenical movement. In order to do so, first we need to understand the Catholic and Orthodox approaches to ecumenism. Second, as students of the icon, we may contribute to that conversation through our respectful understanding of and participation in the iconographic tradition, a participation that may take a variety of forms. Third, we invite others to join that conversation as well. Within the context of this book, the invitations I illustrate primarily focus on students at Mount Angel Seminary, a Catholic seminary in St. Benedict, Oregon. Beyond the seminary, the invitations include materials offered with and to those involved in the Iconographic Arts Institute, as well as presentations and talks for a variety of other groups. These three steps of understanding ecumenism, contributing to the conversation, and inviting others to participate in the conversation correspond to the three parts of this book.

The groups with whom I have been involved each bear some responsibility for gaining a solid understanding of the iconographic tradition. As people who are discerning a vocation as iconographers, the responsibility of the students of the institute to understand and to share the iconographic tradition is clear. Their work and discernment will be deepened through an understanding of the icon's ecumenical implications. Students at Mount Angel Seminary are discerning and studying for the Catholic priesthood. As pastors or from within other leadership positions, they may be called upon to make decisions about the art and environment of their churches and other buildings. If those decisions include traditional iconography, and I hope they do, they need to be shaped by a sound understanding of iconography and Orthodoxy. If they are serving in parishes that commission icons or already have icons in their churches when they arrive, they and their staff will also need to be good stewards of their icons. Good stewardship includes being informed about their icons' theology, aesthetics, and place within the iconographic tradition. Parishes and religious houses in my diocese, the Archdiocese of Portland in Oregon, now have many large icons, thanks to the work of Mary Katsilometes, Kathy Sievers, and a number of their students. These include but are not limited to St. Clare Parish

INTRODUCTION

in Portland, Saint Matthew Catholic Church in Hillsboro, Resurrection Catholic Parish in Tualatin, Our Lady of Guadalupe Trappist Abbey in Lafayette, and Queen of Angels Monastery in Mount Angel. Continuing education about ecumenism, the iconographic tradition, and their specific icons may help people throughout the archdiocese to be good stewards of their icons, as well as perhaps encourage more vocations as iconographers.

The election of Pope Francis as the bishop of Rome gives the ecumenical emphasis of this project additional energy. Ecumenical Patriarch Bartholomew attended the installation of Pope Francis in Rome on March 19, 2013, an action that, according to George E. Demacopolous of the Orthodox Christian Studies Center of Fordham University, "is a profoundly bold step in ecumenical relations between the Orthodox and the Roman Catholics."[2] In response to and in honor of the presence of Patriarch Bartholomew, the Gospel for the installation Mass was chanted in Greek rather than Latin. In his address to Pope Francis the day after the installation, Patriarch Bartholomew emphasized that the unity of the Christian churches is essential to their witness around the world. "We must continue the inaugurated theological dialogue so that we may jointly appreciate and approach the truth of faith, the experience of the saints, and the tradition of the first Christian millennium shared by East and West alike," he said.[3] While that dialogue takes places at the higher and more formal levels of the Roman Catholic Church and the Orthodox Church, the study, work, and prayer that each of us contribute through our own circumstances is also vital.

I am offering a consideration of Orthodoxy and ecumenism, the iconographic tradition, and opportunities for education on these topics that may not have been brought together in one book, particularly for the students and faculties of Catholic seminaries. I also hope I will benefit those discerning a vocation as iconographers and those who have traditional icons in their parishes and religious houses. I hope this work will serve as a complement to the work of Pope Francis and Patriarch Bartholomew and serve as an example of receptive ecumenism.

2. Demacopolous, "Extraordinary Historical Significance," lines 10–11.
3. Bartholomew, "Address by His All-Holiness," lines 11–14.

1

Joining the Conversation
The Ecumenical Movement

The end of each discovery becomes the starting point for the discovery of something higher, and the ascent continues. Thus our ascent is unending. We go from beginning to beginning by way of beginnings without end.

—St. Gregory of Nyssa

Since most members of the intended audience for this project are Catholic Christians, some key documents pertaining to Catholic participation in ecumenism are the entry point for joining the conversation that is the ecumenical movement. These include "Lumen Gentium" and "Unitatis Redintegratio" from among the documents of the Second Vatican Council, the *Directory for the Application of Principles and Norms of Ecumenism*, and John Paul II's *Ut Unum Sint*. Each of these documents is significant for formal and informal students of iconography and thus contributes to their education.

Documents of the Second Vatican Council

Among the sixteen documents of the Second Vatican Council, the constitution "Lumen Gentium: The Dogmatic Constitution on the Church" provides the basic Catholic understanding of the nature of the church that supports the pastoral applications found in the shorter decrees and declarations, including "Unitatis Redintegratio: Decree on Ecumenism." While this discussion focuses on the first chapter of "Lumen Gentium," this constitution also contains sections on the structure of the church, the clergy, laity, and religious, and the eschatological nature of the church.

Toward the end of the first chapter of "Lumen Gentium," the council fathers state that the church "constituted and organized in the world as a society, subsists in the Catholic Church . . . although many elements of sanctification and of truth are found outside of its visible structure."[1] Given this understanding, the spirituality of Christian traditions outside of the Catholic Church may offer fertile ground for Catholics seeking to grow in their faith. This may be particularly true for Catholics who are approaching iconography as an aspect of their prayer or who are discerning a vocation as an iconographer. The icon is an element of sanctification, and Catholics who approach the icon through study and in worship have an opportunity to experience aspects of the Christian tradition they may not currently experience on a regular basis. Icons are certainly found in Catholic parishes and homes, but they often do not have the centrality they have in an Orthodox parish or household. An experience of the fullness of truth found in the Catholic Church is found in the sanctity we experience in the practice of iconography in the Orthodox Church around the world.

The opening chapter of "Lumen Gentium" also calls upon many images from the Scriptures through which Christians may ponder the nature of the church, including the church as a sheepfold, as cultivated land, as the building of God, and as the bride of the Lamb. Two further images from Avery Dulles may also assist us as we join the conversation of the ecumenical movement, particularly with the Orthodox. Avery Dulles's book *Models of the Church*, a classic text in ecclesiology, provides five primary models or images for the church. Dulles discusses the church as institution, the church as mystical communion, the church as sacrament, the church as herald, and the church as servant. In the expanded edition of *Models of the Church*, published in 2002, Dulles includes an additional model, the church as a community of disciples, much of which is based on the writing of John Paul II. While each model has its strengths and weaknesses, for the purposes of conversation with the Orthodox tradition, the models of the church as mystical communion and the church as sacrament may be the most helpful.

---

1 Vatican II, "Lumen Gentium," 130.

The model of the church as mystical communion may also be described as the church as the body of Christ. While this model does not deny the place of the church as an institution with visible structures, it insists that the relationships within the institution "rest upon a deeper spiritual communion of grace or charity."[2] The mystical communion may be considered the soul that animates the body or the institution of the church. The mystical communion, in turn, is animated by the Holy Spirit and includes both the visible and invisible members of the body of Christ, those currently living on earth, as well as all of the just who have gone before them. As indicated in "Lumen Gentium," elements of the mystical communion may be found outside of the Roman Catholic Church; the body of Christ, through the power of the Holy Spirit, may reach beyond its visible structures and traditions.

Dulles points out several advantages of the church as mystical communion, all of which are helpful to Catholics approaching the Orthodox tradition through the study of iconography. This model has solid grounding in the Catholic tradition, including the writings of Saint Augustine and Saint Thomas Aquinas and the documents of the Second Vatican Council, and it can give a renewed energy to living out Christian spirituality today through its emphasis on the communion of saints. The model of the church as a mystical communion also meets "a human need that is acutely experienced by many of the faithful."[3] Large institutions may feel distant and impersonal, leading people to look for places or structures of a more modest, more human, scale. With less focus on an institutional model and the hierarchy that is usually associated with it, the model of the church as mystical communion is "ecumenically very fruitful" since the model of the mystical body of Christ is more "congenial to most Protestants and Orthodox than the institutional model."[4] Overall, this model acknowledges and builds on the real and substantial communion that already exists among Christians from every part of the Christian world.

Dulles also explains that if the model of mystical communion is emphasized too much, it can seem too insubstantial or ethereal with too great a focus on the internal to the detriment of external structures. The pitfall of too much emphasis can affect other models as well, including the institutional model with its focus on the outward and visible organization of the

2. Dulles, *Models of the Church*, 42.
3. Ibid., 51.
4. Ibid., 50.

church. Too much emphasis on the church as institution leads to the neglect of interpersonal relationships. Fortunately, the model of the church as sacrament may ease the tension between these two models of the church as institution and the church as mystical communion. Drawing on the work of Henri de Lubac, Dulles explains that the church as sacrament keeps the divine and human aspects of the church in relationship with one another: "An excessively spiritual and individualistic view of the life of grace . . . leads to a merely secular and sociological understanding of the Church as institution. The notion of sacrament, on the other hand, harmoniously combines both aspects."[5] This harmony can be particularly advantageous for those who are approaching the Orthodox tradition with its rich history of iconography, hymnography, and more physical gestures in prayer and worship.

The model of the church as a sacrament rests on the understanding of a sacrament as an "efficacious sign" that "itself produces or intensifies that of which it is a sign."[6] Christ is the sacrament of God, and the church is the sacrament of Christ that brings the reality of the Incarnation to the world. As it does so, it honors the need for an external structure that provides a means for visible unity and a tangible experience while also pointing toward the spiritual hope and faith of the members of the church. Thus, "the more widely and intensely the faithful participate in this corporate action of the Church, the more the Church achieves itself."[7] While the grace of God is certainly present everywhere, wherever it is present that grace "is in search of a visible form that adequately expresses what it is."[8] This is a fundamental understanding of Christian theology, whether that theology emerges from a Catholic, Reformed, or Orthodox perspective. Those from the Orthodox tradition would point out that while no physical form can contain all of the grace of God, the iconographic tradition offers images and a language whose ability to reveal that grace has endured for millennia.

Dulles discusses several other advantages of the church as sacrament. This model offers a broad definition of witness since it includes every "heartfelt conviction inspired by the grace of the Holy Spirit."[9] The magisterium certainly has a responsibility to guide the expression of those convictions, but their expression does not need to be limited to simply following

---

5. Ibid., 55–56.
6. Ibid., 59.
7. Ibid., 62.
8. Ibid., 64.
9. Ibid.

rules or guidelines. Additionally, those who are recipients of the ministry of the church include anyone who reaches a more complete and lively expression of their faith because of their relationship with the church. The model of the church as sacrament calls for a participation in the life of the church on both the internal and external levels, and those who are clearly involved in both levels would be considered members of the church. However, "even the external spectator," explains Dulles, "especially if he is expectantly looking out for signs of the presence of the revealing God, may catch some of the significance of the Church as a numinous sign."[10] The sacramentality of the icon fits this understanding because the icon may draw its viewers further into the sacrament of Christ and his church, regardless of whether those viewers be Orthodox, Catholic, or from another religious tradition. While those with more understanding of the Christian tradition may be more capable of acting on that experience in a more obviously Christian manner, the grace received by those who do not have that understanding is still real and life-giving.

As seen above, Dulles discusses how each model defines membership in the church. The models of the church as a mystical communion and the church as sacrament offer a less juridical model than the model of the church as institution. The church as institution, particularly an institution with a heavily hierarchical organization, is the model with which most people are familiar and think of when they describe the church. However, an awareness of the variety within institutional organizations is helpful as we approach other Christian traditions, including the Orthodox. This can help Catholics and other Western Christians respect the juridical requirements of the Orthodox while also remaining open to the possibilities offered by the other models described by Dulles.

The second chapter of "Lumen Gentium," entitled "The People of God," outlines the Catholic understanding of membership in the church before it discusses the various components of its organization in the rest of the document. Because the council fathers understand that the church is necessary for salvation, it follows that those who "knowing that the Catholic Church was made necessary by Christ, would refuse to enter or remain in it, could not be saved."[11] Those who recognize the necessity of the church are called to respond to the grace they have received and to persevere in love. The more juridical elements of participating in the sacramental

---

10. Ibid., 65.
11. Vatican II, "Lumen Gentium," 139.

discipline of the church and following its teaching are part of that response, but they are by no means its entirety. An inner response of hope and love is also necessary for salvation; a person who does not respond in such a way "remains indeed in the bosom of the Church, but, as it were, only in a 'bodily' manner and 'not in his heart.'"[12] For those approaching iconography with all of its outward beauty, as well as the bodily gestures that accompany the veneration of an icon, this is an important point to keep in mind. The visible images and actions are important to our membership in the church, for evangelization, and for passing the Christian tradition to future generations. However, our inner conversion is just as important, if not more so. Without that conversion, without that *kenosis*, the outward beauty and gestures lose their meaning.

In its second chapter, "Lumen Gentium" explains the ways in which the Catholic Church recognizes those Christians who are not fully incorporated into the Catholic Church. This portion of the document also fits with Dulles's descriptions of the church as mystical communion and the church as sacrament. Many Christians outside of the Catholic Church are partially united with her through their baptism, their honoring of Scripture, and their prayers to the Father, the Son, and the Holy Spirit. The council fathers teach that all of the disciples of Christ, those within and those outside of the Catholic Church must pursue a desire to be peacefully joined with other Christians.[13] The ecumenical movement cannot truly proceed without that desire on the part of people from the whole spectrum of the Christian tradition as it stands today.

"Lumen Gentium" recognizes that those who have not yet received the gospel are also in relation to the church, that "whatever good or truth is found amongst them is . . . a preparation for the Gospel."[14] Given this, every human being is in some way in relationship with the church, either by persevering in and further deepening his or her commitment as a Christian or by being in the process, recognized and unrecognized, of being called to make such a commitment. Given the attraction, questions, and curiosity that many people express toward iconography, the icon has a place in the development of Christians and non-Christians alike. Questions and curiosity are welcome.

---

12. Ibid.
13. Ibid., 140.
14. Ibid., 141.

A respect for the institutional or juridical model of church, the model of the church as mystical communion, and the model of church as sacrament offer the context in which to discuss another document of the Second Vatican Council, "Unitatis Redintegratio: Decree on Ecumenism." The first sentence of the document from which its title is drawn explains that the "restoration of unity among all Christians is one of the principle concerns of the Second Vatican Council" and thus of the whole church.[15] "Unitatis Redintegratio" acknowledges the longing of many Christians for the healing of divisions among Christians and the desire for some visible form of one church, particularly for the sake of the witness of the church to the rest of the world. It outlines the Catholic principles of ecumenism, the practice of ecumenism that flows from those principles, as well as the special place of the Eastern Churches within ecumenical work and practice. This last point is naturally of particular importance for those pursuing the study of iconography. Despite the divisions, in many ways the Orthodox are the closest brothers and sisters of the Catholic Church because of our shared history, shared theology, and shared liturgical traditions.

Three major principles support all ecumenical work, including the study of iconography. The first principle of ecumenism is the inherent unity of the church, the unity Christ himself prayed for before his passion, death, and resurrection: "I do not pray for these only, but also for those who believe in me through their word, that they may all be one; even as you, Father, are in me, and I in you, that they also may be in us, so that the world may believe that you have sent me."[16] The desire for unity is a desire for the church to be as Christ prayed for it to be, united in mind, heart, and body. The second ecumenical principle is the common baptism in Christ that Catholics share with other Christians. Through "Unitatis Redintegratio" the council fathers teach that "it remains true that all who have been justified by faith in Baptism are members of Christ's body and have a right to be called Christian, and so are correctly accepted as brothers by the children of the Catholic Church."[17] The obstacles that separate other Christians from the Catholic Church are not to be minimized; they are serious. At the same time, the traditions of these Christian brothers and sisters may be a great gift to the Catholic Church and a source of God's grace because "all of these [elements and endowments], which come from Christ and lead

---

15. Vatican II, "Unitatis Redintegratio," 239.
16. John 17:20–21.
17. Vatican II, "Unitatis Redintegratio," 239.

back to Christ, belong by right to the one Church of Christ."[18] Given the shared history of the Orthodox Church and the Catholic Church, this is particularly true of the iconographic tradition, and that tradition should thus be afforded great respect.

The third Catholic ecumenical principle is a shared call to take part in the work of ecumenism. Many Christians around the world have been drawn to ecumenical work, to the practices discussed below that are key ecumenical activities. Those actions, when undertaken with the appropriate guidance of the teachings of the Catholic Church, make a great contribution toward full communion among all Christians. "Unity in essentials" must be preserved, and at the same time the council fathers instruct that "in all things let charity prevail."[19] The faith and actions of our separated brothers and sisters should be given the deepest respect because they are "the riches of Christ and virtuous works in the lives of others who are bearing witness to Christ, sometimes even to the shedding of their blood."[20] As will be discussed below, such martyrs are found in the iconographic tradition, particularly at the time of the iconoclastic controversies and in twentieth-century Russia.

"Unitatis Redintegratio" outlines several practices of ecumenism for Catholic Christians, all of which certainly apply to students of iconography. First is the conversion and renewal of the church itself on the individual and communal levels because "there can be no ecumenism worthy of the name without a change of heart."[21] This can and should take place at various levels within the church. At the level of the individual, we can be committed to a regular examination of conscience and participation in the sacrament of reconciliation. This is an essential part of the spirituality of an iconographer. The desire for unity with our Christian brothers and sisters is one of the many fruits of conversion of the heart, mind, and spirit, "for the closer their [the faithful's] union with the Father, the Word, and the Spirit, the more deeply and easily will they be able to grow in mutual and brotherly love."[22] As Catholics deepen their own conversion, they are able to approach their separated brethren with clearer intentions and understanding.

---

18. Ibid., 243.
19. Ibid., 245.
20. Ibid., 246.
21. Ibid., 247.
22. Ibid., 248.

The second ecumenical practice is common worship in appropriate circumstances and with respect for the liturgical disciplines of all of those involved. Certainly during gatherings with a specifically ecumenical focus, common prayer is appropriate and encouraged, such as during the Week of Christian Unity each January. Two principles guide this worship, that of "bearing witness to the unity of the Church; and second, the sharing in the means of grace."[23] More specific guidance for common worship is given in the *Directory for the Application of Principles and Norms of Ecumenism*.

The last three ecumenical practices address study, presentations of the faith, and cooperation among Christians. Ecumenical study and the awareness of other Christian traditions is important for Christians at every level, from the family home and the local parish to those involved with the church worldwide, and such study at the local level is essential to the success of ecumenical work. Given their leadership roles and responsibilities, the study of the traditions of other Christians, particularly the Orthodox, is important for future priests and other ministers in the Church. They need to gain both historical knowledge and an understanding of theology that may generate respectful relations with sisters and brothers from Christian traditions outside of the Catholic Church. Those who already have a solid Catholic education, whether it has been through Catholic schools, seminary or another means, "need to acquire a more adequate understanding of the respective doctrines of our separated brethren, their history, their spiritual and liturgical life, their religious psychology and general background."[24] This is particularly important if the Catholics involved are entering into a common endeavor with other Christians or drawing on portions of another tradition in some way, such as with iconography and the Orthodox. A lively intellectual and reading life may provide much of this needed background, even when people from various Christian traditions are not readily available for theological conversations.

Fortunately, ecumenical study and awareness may lead to conversations and presentations on religious and theological topics in a variety of settings. "Unitatis Redintegratio" is naturally more concerned with Catholics presenting the Catholic faith. In their discussion of such work, the council fathers teach that the presentations should be clear, accurate, and at the same time "never become an obstacle to dialogue with our brethren."[25] The

---

23. Ibid., 249.
24. Ibid.
25. Ibid., 250.

presentations should be offered in such a way that they are appropriate to the background and abilities of the audience and respect the true meaning of Catholic beliefs and teaching. Catholics also benefit from attending presentations by other Christian traditions, particularly those with whom they are involved through their work or studies. Just as people can learn much by visiting a Catholic parish or attending a talk by local clergy and laity, Catholics can learn much about their fellow Christians by meeting them in their own places of worship and attending their presentations.

The fifth and final principle discussed by "Unitatis Redintegratio" is the cooperation among Christians in a variety of good social works. Such works are a sign of encouragement toward further ecumenical efforts. All of Christ's disciples "can, through this cooperation, be led to acquire better knowledge and appreciation of one another and so pave the way to Christian unity."[26] While all people of good will are called to work together for the good of their communities, this is particularly true of Christians since such work "sets in clearer relief the features of Christ the servant," a Christian spirituality that may be particularly needed and attractive for people today.[27] While all of the practices of ecumenism are important, students of iconography should be particularly mindful of this call to service with other Christians, as well as the call to service in general. Iconography is not just about the pleasure and process of creating beautiful images; it also involves many forms of service. It may involve service to the larger community of iconographers, as well as offering icons and the teaching behind them to individuals and communities that may be unable to pay for or have access to them otherwise.

The final chapter of "Unitatis Redintegratio," entitled "Churches and Ecclesial Communities Separated from the Roman See," includes discussion of the special consideration due to the Eastern Churches. These are the bodies of Christians that were separated from Rome due to divisions related to the Council of Ephesus, the Council of Chalcedon, and later disruptions of communion with the Eastern Patriarchates. They give particular emphasis to their origins with the apostles, an emphasis they share with the Catholic Church. This final chapter outlines several more specific reasons for considering the Orthodox the closest brothers and sisters of the Catholic Church. First and foremost is the shared history between the Eastern Churches and the Roman Catholic Church, particularly "the

26. Ibid.
27. Ibid.

ecumenical councils held in the East that defined the basic dogmas of the Christian faith,"[28] including the dogmas of the Trinity and the Incarnation. That faith has been preserved by the Eastern Churches despite much strife and suffering. The Western tradition is greatly indebted to the theological work done in the East and for many practices of the liturgy and Christian spirituality as well. This is particularly true in the most recent centuries of Christian history, during which the iconographic tradition has been rediscovered in the East and in turn has been taken up by master iconographers and their students in the West.

Second, this final chapter discusses the "very rich liturgical and spiritual heritage of the Eastern Churches" that Catholics should respect and of which they should have a thorough knowledge.[29] In terms of the liturgical traditions, the document notes that the Eastern Churches "possess true sacraments and above all, by apostolic succession, the priesthood and the Eucharist."[30] Therefore, under the appropriate conditions, shared worship is approved of and encouraged by the Catholic Church. Next the document notes the rich monastic tradition that began in the East and was the starting point for monastic life in the West. In ways big and small, these particular points are important for students of iconography. In order to fully understand the place of the icon in Eastern spirituality and liturgy, students need to attend services at an Orthodox parish as often as they can. During the iconoclastic controversies, monks were among the strongest defenders of the icon. In the history of the Iconographic Arts Institute, of which I am a student, such support is manifested through Mount Angel Abbey in St. Benedict, Oregon, and Queen of Angels Monastery in Mount Angel, Oregon. The institute first grew out of an artists' retreat at the abbey and has also been hosted for many years by the sisters at their monastery. In these settings, the students of the institute have been able to take part in the prayer life of the community, particularly the Liturgy of the Hours, while they are pursuing their study of the icon.

Lastly, the document considers the theological tradition of the East, which along with its liturgical and spiritual traditions, belongs to the "full Catholic and apostolic character of the Church."[31] The Eastern theological tradition has developed through the study of Scripture and been brought

---

28. Ibid., 252.
29. Ibid., 253.
30. Ibid.
31. Ibid., 254.

to bear on its deep liturgical tradition and the work of its many spiritual writers. Through this work, the East has often developed theological expressions that significantly differ from those of the West. However, "Unitatis Redintegratio" affirms that "from time to time one tradition has come nearer to a full appreciation of some aspects of a mystery of revelation . . . or has expressed it to better advantage."[32] This statement encourages the engagement with another tradition that is key to receptive ecumenism, which will be discussed below. It supports our learning of the iconographic tradition and points us toward the necessary humility that allows us to take in as much of that tradition as possible.

Directory for the Application of Principles and Norms of Ecumenism

"Lumen Gentium" and "Unitatis Redintegratio" give Catholic students of iconography the basic framework for their engagement with the Orthodox tradition, and the models of the church as mystical communion and the church as sacrament support a vision of the church that more easily includes our Orthodox brothers and sisters. The next document, the *Directory for the Application of Principles and Norms of Ecumenism* from the Pontifical Council for Promoting Christian Unity, outlines the actions that follow through on the principles outlined in "Lumen Gentium" and "Unitatis Redintegratio." It clarifies which actions are appropriate for Catholics as they engage in ecumenical work, and according to the editors of *Introduction to Ecumenism*, gives "a coherent view of the institutional and theological commitment of the Church to the ecumenical movement."[33] Because of that coherence and the additional detail it offers, the *Directory* is a vital document for those engaging with the Orthodox tradition through their study of iconography, particularly the sections of the *Directory* discussed below.

Right from the outset, the *Directory* points out that the secular culture that currently surrounds so many Christians "calls Christians to common action in their hope for the Kingdom of God."[34] While the differences among Christian communities should not be minimized, their common commitment to Jesus Christ can help counter the secular culture. The *Directory* supports common action by establishing the norms that order the relations

32. Ibid.
33. Gros et al., *Introduction to Ecumenism*, 48.
34. Pontifical Council for Promoting Christian Unity, *Directory*, 14.

between Catholics and other Christians so that common action will be consistent with the documents of the Second Vatican Council.

The first chapter of the *Directory*, entitled "The Search for Christian Unity," explains that Catholics need to know their own tradition and its principles of ecumenism so they can engage in accurate discussions with other Christians. This book is, in part, an effort to bring those principles to those with an interest in Orthodox iconography. Knowing one's own tradition includes knowing how the local diocese organizes its ecumenical work through its ecumenical officer and ecumenical commission, as well as gaining familiarity with other efforts taken up by the laity or local apostolic or monastic communities. As students of the icon pursue their studies, the instruction to understand their own tradition applies more broadly as well. As they study the iconographic tradition of the East, knowledge of the history of art in the West is also helpful. The context that knowledge provides can keep students from considering the icon in isolation from larger movements in art and history.

The *Directory* also explains that the ecumenical situation will differ according to each community and each Catholic's situation; therefore, "the particular local context will always furnish the different characteristics of the ecumenical task."[35] For iconography students, while this context includes the broader traditions of the East from which they are learning, it also includes the Orthodox churches in their local area. If we consider just the United States, the history of Orthodoxy differs depending on which area of the country is under consideration. The Ancient Faith Radio podcast entitled *American Orthodox History*, for example, can offer good material and insights on this point. An understanding of the various Orthodox jurisdictions, which to a non-Orthodox Christian can be quite confusing, is also essential to understanding the context of one's local Orthodox parishes.

In the section entitled "Ecumenical Formation in the Catholic Church," the *Directory* explains that all of the faithful "are called upon to make a personal commitment toward increasing communion with other Christians."[36] This includes having a good understanding of the ecumenical principles of the Church as discussed in "Lumen Gentium" and "Unitatis Redintegratio." Two other points from this section are particularly pertinent for the seminary students and faculty. In terms of the formation of seminarians, the *Directory* states that their seminary course on ecumenism

---

35. Ibid., 24.
36. Ibid., 37.

"might include the need for better knowledge of Eastern theology and spirituality."[37] Beyond their course on ecumenism, this need may be met by pertinent presentations in other courses, as well as elective courses in Eastern theology and iconography.

The *Directory* also dedicates a portion of this section to teachers and other personnel involved in pastoral ministries; they have a particular responsibility to have a solid ecumenical commitment. That commitment should be formed through a number of "principle orientations."[38] In terms of study, these orientations including knowledge of the Scriptures and Catholic doctrine, a knowledge of church history that includes the history of the divisions within Christianity, and knowledge of the results of ecumenical dialogues. With this background, teachers and ministers can steer away from incorrect interpretations of Catholicism and other Christian traditions. Overall, their ecumenical formation brings together all areas of the Christian world, making "concern for the unity of the Catholic Church and concern for communion with other Churches and ecclesial communities inseparable."[39] Their pastoral concern and knowledge becomes an ecumenical work itself.

Those involved in the study of iconography and who visit Eastern Orthodox churches on a regular basis need to be familiar with the guidelines provided in the *Directory* that cover sharing the sacramental life with members of the Eastern Orthodox churches. The first step is locating the Orthodox communities in a given area, which is easily done with several directories that are available online. The *Directory* first points out the grounds for common worship from "Unitatis Redintegratio" that are discussed above. Because the Catholic Church understands the Eastern Churches to possess true sacraments, there are legitimate grounds for some sharing in liturgical worship. However, "on the basis of their own ecclesiological understanding, [Eastern Churches] may have more restrictive disciplines in this matter, which others should respect."[40] Because Catholics are guests of another community when they attend an Orthodox parish, it is imperative that we respect their sacramental discipline. "A Catholic who legitimately wishes to communicate with Eastern Christians," explains the *Directory*, "must refrain from communicating if that Church restricts sacramental

37. Ibid., 49.
38. Ibid., 38.
39. Ibid.
40. Ibid., 67.

communion to its own members to the exclusion of others."[41] To attempt to do otherwise could create scandal and alienation that is contrary to true communion and ecumenical work.

The *Directory* explains that a Catholic may request the sacrament of reconciliation, eucharistic communion, or the anointing of the sick from a minister of an Orthodox Church if it is impossible for them to be served by a member of the Catholic clergy. If a Catholic takes communion in an Eastern church, they should also respect that church's discipline regarding confession prior to communion, the eucharistic fast, and the frequency of communion. Overall, even though the desire for sacramental communion with our Orthodox brothers and sisters can certainly be part of our prayer for the unity of all Christians, we should not take part in that sacramental communion until a more visible and formal unity between the Roman Catholic Church and the Orthodox Church has been established.

In its final section, entitled "Ecumenical Cooperation: Dialogue and Common Witness," the points made in the *Directory* that are directly applicable to Catholic seminaries are in the subsection entitled "Cooperation in Institutes of Higher Studies." In terms of undergraduate seminary studies, the *Directory* indicates "in accordance with the general criteria for the ecumenical formation of Catholic students," students may attend courses or institutes with an ecumenical focus.[42] When they are available, institutes that focus on the icon and other liturgical arts may present a great opportunity for such study, for those interested in theology as well as those who are also interested in the craft and technique of iconography. More sophisticated ecumenical study and contributions are possible at the graduate and postgraduate levels since the students and faculty have a more solid grounding in their own faith. Contributions may occur through sharing research with colleagues from other Christian communities, consulting with colleagues on research in progress, collaborative research, and administering or teaching in ecumenical institutions.

Lastly, as students of the icon get to know the Orthodox communities and parishioners in their areas, the opportunity for some common witness and missionary activities may arise. Even with the current divisions among Christians, Christian communities can still offer a common witness to the gospel that may encourage secular society to look at the Christian faith anew. The ministry and mission of the icon can certainly

41. Ibid.
42. Ibid., 89.

be part of that witness. The icon has work to do in a world starved for balance, calm, and beauty.

Ut Unum Sint: On Commitment to Ecumenism and Additional Contributions

While the *Directory* provides concrete norms for ecumenical work, *Ut Unum Sint*, the encyclical letter of John Paul II that was published in 1995, two years after the *Directory*, adds to those norms material that focuses more on relations with the Churches in the East. According to the editors of *Introduction to Ecumenism*, *Ut Unum Sint: On Commitment to Ecumenism* gives "rigor and specificity to the ecumenical movement, to complement the more institutional tone of the *Directory*."[43] After the first chapter, in which he affirms the commitment of the Catholic Church to ecumenism, John Paul II uses chapter 2 to discuss the fruits of the ecumenical dialogues, which by that point had taken place since the Second Vatican Council.

The first of those fruits is a rediscovery of a common Christian bond, one of a "fraternal charity that embraces all Christ's disciples."[44] He notes a change in language: rather than referring to "separated brethren" we may speak of these groups as, for instance, "others who have received Baptism."[45] While not ignoring the legitimate differences among various groups of Christians, and even the aggression that they can direct toward one another, this change in language does indicate a shifting attitude toward other Christians. Shared service and mission, the second fruit, builds on that understanding of shared discipleship. This service includes offering a collective Christian voice that speaks to and supports the dignity of every human person.

John Paul II also discusses a few details of the ecumenical work that has been accomplished in terms of Scripture and the liturgy. Ecumenical translations of the Bible "offer a solid basis for the prayer and pastoral activity of all Christ's followers."[46] Given the role played by divisions about Scripture in the broken communion among Christians in the West, this is particularly significant. Additionally, other Christians in the West have given attention to liturgical renewal, particularly in terms of celebrating

43. Gros et al., *Introduction to Ecumenism*, 50.
44. John Paul II, *Ut Unum Sint*, 49.
45. Ibid., 48.
46. Ibid., 52.

the Lord's Supper, revising the cycles of their lectionaries, and giving more prominence to "liturgical signs (images, icons, vestments, lights, incense, gestures)."[47] This interest is evident in groups such as the Iconographic Arts Institute, which draws students from a range of Christian denominations. Lastly, work and friendships with other Christians since the Second Vatican Council have enabled Catholics to recognize and understand how God is working in the lives of other Christians and their communities, including ways that lead to martyrdom for the faith around the world.[48] Their witness contributes to the deepening of our own faith.

With the section in *Ut Unum Sint* on the fruits of ecumenical dialogue, John Paul II devotes a significant amount of space to the dialogue between the Roman Catholic Church and the Eastern Orthodox Church. He mentions several significant events that have been part of the two bodies approaching one another with a renewed sense of common discipleship: the lifting of the mutual excommunications of 1054 by Pope Paul VI and Ecumenical Patriarch Athenagoras, the celebration in 1984 of the eleventh centenary of Saints Cyril and Methodius and his proclamation of the Apostles to the Slavs as co-patrons of Europe, and the celebration of the Millennium of the Baptism of Rus' in 1988.[49] He also discusses the Joint International Commission for the Theological Dialogue between the Catholic Church and the Orthodox Church, which was established in 1979. Those dialogues have been "slow and arduous," John Paul II explains, "yet a source of great joy; and it has been inspiring, for it has led to the gradual rediscovery of brotherhood."[50] John Paul II explains how key understandings in that dialogue laid the groundwork for continuing the discussion. These understandings include a shared and fundamental faith in the mystery of the church, the sacraments, and the essential place of apostolic succession.[51] While, as John Paul II explains, the process is slow, the commission has also been addressing how to reestablish full communion between the Roman Catholic Church and the Eastern Orthodox Church.

Ecumenical developments with all of the Eastern Churches are also discussed in the book *Introduction to Ecumenism*. This book, edited by Jeffrey Gros, Eamon McManus, and Ann Riggs, is an excellent presentation of

47. Ibid.
48. Ibid., 55.
49. Ibid., 60–62.
50. Ibid., 58.
51. Ibid., 69.

the history and theology of ecumenism, Catholic ecumenical principles and formation, and the nature of ecumenical dialogue. The latter chapters of the book discuss the ecumenical dialogues the Roman Catholic Church has had with various communities of Christians, including the Eastern Churches. Thus, in addition to the information it provides about the ecumenical work done between the Roman Catholic Church and the Eastern Churches, it offers students and seminarians, iconographers, and pastors and other ministers a worldwide overview of ecumenical work and relations.

The editors of *Introduction to Ecumenism* discuss all of the Eastern Churches, in keeping with their focus on the entire Christian world. Here we will focus on the dialogue between the Roman Catholic Church and the Eastern Orthodox Church. The editors first explain that different understandings of what constitutes the divisions between East and West need to be understood in order to join the conversation. While Latin Catholics tend to see the divisions between East and West as one of schism, "the Orthodox tend to consider it a matter of doctrine."[52] Nationality and ethnic backgrounds are also important considerations as Latin Catholics seek greater understanding of the Orthodox Church. While "Eastern Orthodoxy has condemned ethnocentric reductionism as heretical," each nationality also has a rich tradition that may be a barrier to fuller understanding with Latin Catholics and even other Orthodox.[53] The Eastern Churches understand the Catholic Church to have separated itself from the tradition it shares with the East. Historically, the main events of that separation, the excommunication of 1054 and the Fourth Crusade and sack of Constantinople in 1204, support this understanding of the actions of the Catholic Church.[54]

While terms such as "schismatic" and "heretic" have been used in the past, they are seldom used by Latin Catholics in the present.[55] Hopefully, this is particularly the case when Catholics have been taught the proper definition of these terms. Within the curriculum of Mount Angel Seminary, Dr. Shawn Keough has offered his students in the graduate history course on the Middle Ages clear definitions of these and two other important and related terms. First, he explains that heretics can only come from within the community of baptized Christians; a non-Christian is a nonbeliever, not a heretic. Heresy is also the obstinate denial of a

---

52. Gros et al., *Introduction to Ecumenism*, 154.
53. Ibid., 155.
54. Ibid., 163.
55. Ibid., 155.

fundamental teaching of the Church. Struggling with doubt or questions does not make a Christian a heretic, so long as he remains in conversation with the Church. Additionally, a theologian or other person who willingly submits their work to the judgment of the Church is not a heretic because through that submission, the person remains in conversation with the authority of the Church's teaching.[56]

Heresy must also be differentiated from incredulity, apostasy, and schism. A person who commits incredulity neglects revealed truth; he or she knows that a teaching of the Church is true but refuses to acknowledge it as such. Even a person who becomes a heretic does not go as far as a person who commits apostasy. While a heretic struggles with portions of the faith, apostasy occurs when one of the baptized completely renounces the entire faith.[57] Lastly, and unlike heresy, incredulity, and apostasy, schism concerns the unity of the Church rather than dogma and is defined as the refusal of submission or communion, particularly with the pope.[58]

The editors of *Introduction to Ecumenism* note a number of other aspects of the current relationship between the Roman Catholic Church and the Orthodox Church of which students of ecumenism need to be aware, and the same may be said of those studying iconography in a seminary or in another setting. These other aspects include the political histories and current situations of Eastern Europe and the Middle East, as well as the theological point of view of Mount Athos that often stands opposed to the modern ecumenical movement. An awareness of these issues will help iconography students and seminarians to handle the iconographic tradition with increased sensitivity. It will also help them understand that like Catholicism, the world of Orthodoxy is not monolithic but contains many points of view, some of which are more supportive of their work with iconography and some of which are not. The editors of *Introduction to Ecumenism* also indicate that study of the responses from the Orthodox observers at the Second Vatican Council and the relationship that has developed between the Roman Catholic Church and the Orthodox Church through the World Council of Churches is helpful.

As mentioned above, the mutual lifting of the excommunications of East and West by Pope Paul VI and Patriarch Athenagoras in 1965 started the contemporary process of dialogue and reconciliation between the

---

56. Shawn Keough, Middle Ages lecture for Mount Angel Seminary, February 2012.
57. Ibid.
58. Ibid.

Catholic Church and the Eastern Orthodox Church. Following this important event, a dialogue of charity that involved exchanging representatives on the Feast of St. Andrew and the Feast of St. Paul took place for fifteen years. Then a dialogue of truth, a more specifically theological dialogue, began in 1980.[59] The dialogue has proceeded by first focusing on those areas in which both the Catholics and the Orthodox agree, with the hope that those areas will provide a sound basis for discussion of more difficult areas that divide the churches. *Introduction to Ecumenism* offers a summary of the major documents resulting from this dialogue, while also explaining that "a more careful study of the texts themselves and of the events of history will be necessary to penetrate the importance and depth of this relationship and its challenges."[60] This would also be another useful portion of study for Catholic seminarians and other students of iconography.

Thus far, the dialogue of truth has issued three major documents. The first document was completed in 1982 and is entitled "The Mystery of the Church and of the Eucharist in the Light of the Mystery of the Holy Trinity." It outlines common convictions about the Trinity, the Eucharist, and the episcopate. These convictions provide the basis on which further dialogue concerning the roles of councils, patriarchs, and popes, as well as the *filioque*, may take place.[61] A second, shorter document was completed in 1987 and is entitled "Faith, Sacraments, and the Unity of the Church." It describes the sacraments in Catholic and Orthodox practice and the differences between the two. The editors of *Introduction to Ecumenism* state that while the end of the document suggests that a diversity of practice in the sacraments of initiation need not necessarily be an impediment to mutual recognition of the sacraments of initiation, "the Statement stops short of making a specific judgment concerning the legitimacy of the present differences in practice."[62] Therefore, a statement concerning recognition of one another's sacraments was not included in the document.

The third document was completed in 1988 and is entitled "The Sacrament of Orders in the Sacramental Structure of the Church, with Particular Reference to the Importance of Apostolic Succession for the Sanctification and Unity of the People of God." This document looks at the means by which communion and communication among the churches has been

---

59. Gros et al., *Introduction to Ecumenism*, 164.
60. Ibid.
61. Ibid., 66.
62. Ibid., 167.

lived, with a focus on the council of bishops and the place of the head of the council. More work had been planned by the dialogue, which was to result in another document entitled "Ecclesiological and Canonical Consequences of the Sacramental Structure of the Church: Conciliarity and Authority in the Church." However, the question of uniatism became more important due to the political realities in the former Soviet Union and Eastern Europe.[63] Therefore, in 1993 the Catholic-Orthodox dialogue issued a statement entitled "Uniatism, Method of Union in the Past, and the Present Search for Full Communion." Uniatism is the practice of communities of Orthodox Christians putting themselves in union with the bishop of Rome while retaining all of their Orthodox liturgical practices and traditions. Referring to communities as "uniate" is now considered a derogatory term that implies force and betrayal. The statement explains that uniatism is not a constructive method for obtaining unity and is no longer an acceptable practice. It also, however, respects the history that has already transpired by acknowledging the place Eastern Catholic Churches have in addressing the needs of many of the faithful. The document also expresses the hope that Oriental Catholic Churches can be constructively brought into the dialogue.[64] The statement concludes by renouncing the desire on the part of the Catholic Church for its expansion to the detriment of the Orthodox Church and with the hope that those autocephalous churches that were not yet a part of the dialogue would take part in the future.[65]

The editors of *Introduction to Ecumenism* explain that the dialogue's document on uniatism has received various levels of acceptance within the Orthodox and Eastern Catholic Churches, which seems to indicate that uniatism is still a sensitive and difficult issue and one of which Catholic seminarians and students of the icon need to be aware, particularly as they encounter Eastern Catholic Churches. Lastly, in addition to the work done on this statement, a theological dialogue between Eastern Orthodox Churches and the Catholic Church has been held in the United States for more than thirty years. Fortunately, that dialogue has proceeded even when international meetings between the two churches were not possible.[66]

As the editors of *Introduction to Ecumenism* point out, a portion of the reform of the Catholic Church since the Second Vatican Council has

---

63. Ibid., 168.
64. Ibid.
65. Ibid.
66. Ibid., 169.

been the rediscovery of the "Eastern dimension of the common Tradition, and an appreciation of traditions that complement its own."[67] This is a key development upon which the study of iconography by seminarians and all Roman Catholics rests. As I engage in the study and practice of iconography and share that study with others, we are furthering this rediscovery and love for our common Christian tradition. In order to truly appreciate those traditions they must be approached with respect and humility, with love. Part of that work is also developing an understanding of where ecumenical dialogue currently stands between the Roman Catholic Church and the Eastern Orthodox Churches. As the bishops and theologians work at their level on the dialogue of truth, we can all do our part in the dialogue of love that supports the dialogue of truth.

Ecumenism, by the very fact that it exists, indicates a sense of incompleteness, of being in process. The final section of this chapter offers some additional sources from those within the Catholic Church who have been responsible for guiding the work of ecumenism and that can help to provide the underpinnings for the current and future ecumenical work of which the study of the icon is a part. The first is a talk given by Cardinal Johannes Willebrands, a past president of the then Vatican Secretariat for Promoting Christian Unity, now the Pontifical Council for Promoting Christian Unity. While his talk was given in 1985, many of its points about the reception of the ecumenical movement itself are still pertinent. The ecumenical movement, he explains, "should be accepted, confirmed and 'received' by all Christians."[68] In order for that reception to occur fully and accurately, education about the above principles and practices of ecumenism is necessary. Catholics, particularly seminarians, clergy, and others who serve the faithful, and other Christians should understand that ecumenism can be hard and uncomfortable work. In terms of iconography, Willebrands's statement implies that those learning about the iconographic tradition need to take up ecumenism as an essential part of their work. Failing to do so may weaken the understanding of students of the icon who do not come from within the Orthodox tradition.

Willebrands explains some of the details of the concept of reception through which we can also examine the work of a Catholic seminarian studying iconography as well as Catholic iconographers. Reception, he explains, is a work of the magisterium and of all of the people. Reception is

67. Ibid.
68. Willebrands, "Impact," 721.

a process through which the Holy Spirit guides the entire Church so that she "recognizes and accepts new insights, new witnesses of truth and their forms of expression because they are deemed to be in the line of the apostolic tradition and in harmony with the *sensus fidelium* of the church as a whole."[69] Sometimes reception refers primarily to official doctrine, but it can also include other aspects of the life of the Church, including liturgy, the spiritual life, and moral questions.[70] While iconography has always been a part of the shared Christian tradition as a whole, there is a sense in which the iconographic tradition needs to be and is being re-received in the West. The material itself is not new, but its renewed place in the liturgical and spiritual traditions in the West is, and its re-reception can weave it once again more fully into the life of the Church. This re-reception of the iconographic tradition does not need to be a replica of how that tradition was played out in the past. Rather, with full acknowledgment of the history and changes that have transpired, it can find a place that honors the Orthodox tradition while also acknowledging the new physical and communal contexts into which iconography may fit into the life of Catholic parishes, schools, seminaries and other settings today.

Cardinal Willebrands also explains that all of the charisms and services within the Church play a part in the process of reception: theologians by their research, the faithful by their fidelity, and the ecclesial ministries, especially the bishops, through their binding decisions. Thus everyone in the Church is involved in learning and reflecting on the ecumenical movement and the issues, challenges, and joys that it entails. This learning involves more than just the theological documents issued by the Church and the ecumenical dialogues. According to Cardinal Willebrands, it also involves developments in the liturgy, pastoral care, and forms of piety, all three of which do or may significantly involve iconography. Cardinal Willebrands points out that from the moment in time in which this article was published, twenty years after the close of the Second Vatican Council, many of the current priests, teachers, and parents were small children at the time of the council.[71] Of course from the vantage point of today, over fifty years after the council, two generations of priests, teachers, and parents were not even born at the time of council. Therefore, the understanding of the ecumenical movement that has grown out of the council must continue to be

69. Ibid., 722.
70. Ibid.
71. Ibid., 723.

taught, and not just in seminaries or other institutions of higher education, but in contexts such as the Iconographic Arts Institute where the students and teachers are drawing from the larger Christian tradition and introducing it into areas of the life of the Church from which it has been largely absent or perhaps misunderstood.

In addition to the remarks of Cardinal Willebrands, an understanding of spiritual ecumenism moves the ecumenical work of the icon forward. Spiritual ecumenism is conversion of our own hearts, the search for holiness, and our prayers for the unity we seek. It is entering more fully and consciously into those areas that cause tension and conflict and a willingness to live with that conflict rather than resolving it prematurely. As the editors of *Introduction to Ecumenism* explain, "What often presents itself as a pastoral moment of tension is an invitation to ecumenical formation and deepening of mutual understanding."[72] For instance, I was approached about the possibility of writing an icon of Mother Maria Brunner, the founder of the Sisters of the Precious Blood. While the community eventually decided to put the project on hold, my initial conversations with their superior brought forth questions I would need to address when considering an icon of a modern personage, as well as of a person who has not been officially canonized.

In his small book *A Handbook of Spiritual Ecumenism*, Cardinal Walter Kasper, also a past president of the Pontifical Council for Promoting Christian Unity, offers numerous suggestions for activities which Christians may constructively and prayerfully pursue together, and iconography can easily be incorporated into many of these projects. For instance, under the section entitled "Deepening Christian Faith," he includes a subsection on common Bible work grounded in the reverence all Christians have for the Scriptures, which are first and foremost met in liturgy and further opened by good preaching.[73] As Cardinal Kasper explains, Scripture "strengthens the life of the faithful, as 'food for the soul' and 'source of spiritual life.'"[74] Icons are commonly referred to as the Scriptures in line and color; thus icons can be easily incorporated into the programs and Bible study resources Kasper encourages his readers to develop. This could be done in simple ways, such as a short presentation on an icon that depicts the biblical passage or theological concept that is the subject of a Bible study or reflection

---

72. Gros et al., *Introduction to Ecumenism*, 85.
73. Kasper, *Handbook*, 20.
74. Ibid.

on a given day. For instance, the icon of the Mother of God of the Sign is a representation of the passage from the prophet Isaiah that is so prominent in Advent: "Behold, a virgin shall conceive and bear a son, and shall call his name Emmanuel."[75] Time with this image, either in silent prayer or through its incorporation into a larger discussion, would be beneficial for any Bible study during Advent.

In Kasper's next section, entitled "Prayer and Worship," iconography may be incorporated into his suggestions under the subsection "The Liturgical Year," particularly if a portion of the program or reflection provides some explanation of the icon in question. Because many Christians in the West, including seminarians, lack the vocabulary for understanding the visual imagery of an icon, providing some basic information can remove some of the puzzlement that may stand in the way of prayer and reflection. An example of such a presentation on the Last Judgment is provided below in chapter 3. Other examples include icons of John the Baptist during Advent and the festal icon of the Nativity of the Lord throughout the octave of Christmas. During Holy Week, icons of the Crucifixion and the Resurrection could be explicated. The celebration of All Saints' Day could involve the participants exploring the icons of various saints of their own choosing. The possibilities are endless.

In addressing the celebrations from throughout the year that are specific to particular communities of Christians, Cardinal Kasper mentions the Sunday of Orthodoxy, the first Sunday of Lent in the Orthodox Church.[76] This is an excellent point in the liturgical year for Catholics to learn about the iconographic canon and to also explore why that canon is so essential to Orthodox theology and spirituality. The Sunday of Orthodoxy commemorates not just the end of the iconoclastic controversies but the triumph of the belief in the Incarnation, in God becoming a man. As Cardinal Kasper mentions, this celebration is an excellent opportunity for spiritual ecumenism, for prayer for the restoration of visible unity between the Roman Catholic Church and the Orthodox Church.

Lastly, in his section entitled "'*Diakonia*' and Witness," Cardinal Kasper discusses the roles of various groups within the Church in supporting and taking part in spiritual ecumenism.[77] Under the section on monastic communities, he explains that they can be centers of prayer for Christian unity

75. Isa 7:14.

76. Kasper, *Handbook*, 69.

77. Ibid., 82.

and places of hospitality for those outside of the community who wish to gather as Christians of different backgrounds. Of course many monasteries have rich traditions of doing so through the people they welcome in their guest houses and retreat centers. With the Iconographic Arts Institute, the connection with monastic communities has been essential, as it started as a program offered by Mount Angel Abbey in St. Benedict, Oregon, and has been hosted by Queen of Angels Monastery in Mount Angel, Oregon, for the last twelve years. Kasper also mentions that monastic communities can "promote joint studies and publications on the major figures of monasticism in both East and West, and on their spiritual teaching."[78] Such works can certainly be the creation or commissioning of icons, written materials to accompany particular icons, and studies of the practice and vocation of monks who are also iconographers. For instance, Queen of Angels Monastery has two large icons written through the hands of the students and instructors of the Iconographic Arts Institute, one of the Transfiguration and one of the Protecting Veil of the Mother of God. Part of spiritual ecumenism in that context could be developing more materials to support the good stewardship of these images and to facilitate hospitality toward those who visit the chapel and spend time with these icons.

Receptive Ecumenism and Catholic Learning

The concept of spiritual ecumenism is the bedrock of ecumenical work today. Ecumenical work must be grounded in prayer, our own conversion, and the conversion of our home communities. The concept of receptive ecumenism will add more weight to the work of spiritual ecumenism, as well as provide some of the theoretical framework for the activities described in chapter 3. As we receive the ecumenical movement itself, we also receive the history and traditions of other Christians, and receptive ecumenism offers a way to describe that process of learning and sharing the fruits of that study and contemplation. It gives us a framework for addressing the messy nature of approaching other traditions and of always being in the midst of the process of learning, receiving, and asking the next question.

The term "receptive ecumenism" derives from the Receptive Ecumenism project, a project of the Centre for Catholic Studies at Durham University. The driving principle behind the project is the humility and

78. Ibid.

openness that is necessary for engaging with other Christian traditions. With ecumenical work and study, we begin from a place in which we ask what we need to learn from other traditions rather than what other traditions first need to learn from us before our relations with other Christians can move forward.[79] The underlying assumption of this approach is that if all of the people involved in ecumenical work and study took on this stance and took it seriously, they would understand their own identity more fully and be engaged in more profound learning and more profound relationships with other Christians.

The first phase of the project consisted of an international research colloquium entitled Catholic Learning and Receptive Ecumenism that was held at Durham University in 2006. The task of the colloquium was to "explore a fresh way of conceiving the ecumenical task fitted for the contemporary situation."[80] The colloquium resulted in the publication of the book *Receptive Ecumenism and the Call to Catholic Learning: Exploring a Way for Contemporary Ecumenism*, from which much of the material for this section is drawn. I have primarily drawn from the first part of the volume entitled "Vision and Principles." Receptive ecumenism builds on the work of spiritual ecumenism and widens ecumenical work and study by bringing together individual commitment and larger institutional structures. It allows groups that are committed to its process to bring ecumenism into their work and their concrete thinking, as well as their prayer and spirituality.

At the beginning of "Vision and Principles," Paul D. Murray discusses several presuppositions that support the work of receptive ecumenism and Catholic learning. The first, the ecclesial-theological presuppositions, explain that a primary assumption of receptive ecumenism is that "the life of faith, personally, communally—or, better, ecclesially—is always in essence a matter of becoming more fully, more richly, what we already are."[81] Individually and communally, we are made in the image and likeness of God, and we are always growing toward a more complete realization of that reality. As challenging as the differences among Christian traditions and communities may be, we do have a shared Christian identity. As we grow

---

79. Centre for Catholic Studies, Durham University, "Receptive Ecumenism," updated July 12, 2018, https://www.dur.ac.uk/theology.religion/ccs/constructivetheology/receptiveecumensim.

80. Centre for Catholic Studies, Durham University, "Project 1: Receptive Ecumenism," updated July 11, 2018, https://www.dur.ac.uk/theology.religion/ccs/projects/receptiveecumenism/projects/catholiclearning/.

81 Murray, "Receptive Ecumenism," 6.

through our ecumenical work, we maintain our Christian identity across time yet also make appropriate changes "when occasion demands, [doing] genuinely fresh things yet in familiar or recognizably coherent ways."[82] Those changes should be life-giving to the Church, and ecumenical work and study is an especially rich place from which such changes and greater communion may emerge.

Next Murray explains some cultural-intellectual presuppositions for the Receptive Ecumenism and Catholic Learning Project. Receptive ecumenism assumes that human reason is "always starting in the middle of things, already shaped by inherited stances, assumptions, values, and received knowledge, all with varying levels of associated significance and embeddedness."[83] From that middle, from their own thoughtful understanding of their situation, those involved in receptive ecumenism give their own context its proper respect, a respect that in no way diminishes the truth of that context or one's commitment to that truth. At the same time, we are "continually opening it [our tradition] out to testing against what else there is and what comes to light."[84] Taking up a process such as this is not easy or comfortable. Murray describes this as the position of a "committed pluralist,"[85] a term that implies a tension that must be lived and questioned rather than prematurely resolved or, worse, ignored. At the same time, it also implies an active interest in the experience of Christian communities outside of those in which we were raised or chose for ourselves later in our lives.

Third, Murray discusses the current ecclesial-historical context in the section entitled "Anticipating Spring in a Wintry Season." First Murray acknowledges that "the ecumenical aspiration for forms of theological, practical, and structural unity . . . will necessarily be a long haul."[86] This is not, however, a sound reason for stepping away from serious questions or for disengaging from difficult conversations. "What is the appropriate ethic," Murray asks, "between the times in relation to this [ecumenical] calling?"[87] He compares the possibility of giving up on ecumenism to giving up on economic justice because we will never fully achieve it for everyone. Our

82. Ibid., 7.
83. Ibid., 8.
84. Ibid.
85. Ibid.
86. Ibid., 12.
87. Ibid.

contributions may seem and may in fact be a very small part of the work that constitutes that long haul, even when that work contains sound questions, thorough research, and thoughtful reflection. Receptive ecumenism seeks to make contributions to ecumenical projects without a distracting concern for the place it has within the larger scheme of ecumenical work.

Murray and his colleagues explain that the strategies of receptive ecumenism are not a replacement for the more conceptual and theological work that is already taking place but are a necessary part of that work. He assumes that receptive ecumenism has "the potential to take each tradition with integrity"[88] to a different place than it is now. Within those new places, each Christian tradition may find itself in circumstances in which differences that seemed insurmountable before "become genuinely navigable as all grow with creative integrity but non-linearly" beyond the question at hand that may have seemed overwhelming before taking up receptive ecumenism.[89] Our understanding is expanded as each tradition moves into their learning honorably and with great care. While it takes place at a different level, the learning done through receptive ecumenism is not a second-rate process, a task unequal to the important work of conceptual clarity, but "the essential way forward towards the anticipated goal of organic structural unity."[90] Without the learning that is encouraged by receptive ecumenism, attempts at such structural unity would perhaps seem hollow, unsupported, and ultimately fail.

Within the educational ethic of receptive ecumenism, learning takes precedence over teaching. Each tradition is responsible for its own learning and understanding of other traditions; people within each tradition must be willing to invest energy and interest in the history, theology, and spirituality of other Christians. As each tradition does so, it is "willing to facilitate the learning of others as requested but without requiring how this should be done, or even making others' learning a precondition to attending to one's own."[91] Essentially, the learning of individuals within each tradition is not dependent on the willingness of particular individuals within other traditions to teach them or to even recognize their willingness to learn. The learning moves forward in whatever way it can, through whatever means and people are available at the time. More reciprocal learning is desirable;

---

88. Ibid., 14.
89. Ibid.
90. Ibid., 15.
91. Ibid.

however, there isn't any reason to allow a lack of reciprocity to stop or even slow down our research and projects. In this way, receptive ecumenism is realistic about the barriers that exist among communities without becoming dismayed by them.

Receptive ecumenism, particularly taking responsibility for one's own learning, resonates with my philosophy of teaching. Receptive ecumenism offers a mode of learning that becomes itself a form of teaching. Rather than "repeating, judging and defending" as we work within our Christian tradition, this model teaches us to offer our work "in the mode of witness—arguably the most authentic form of Christian teaching."[92] Of course there are times when a vigorous defense of a particular belief is necessary; this model should not fall into a failure to recognize and speak to the truth. It does, however, stand in the reality of the power of actions as well as words. In the end, receptive ecumenism is a way of working and thinking that may be of help to far more than the ecumenical movement. It supports all of those areas that seem to have intractable differences, where a stance of learning is in fact a way of witnessing to our desire to remain within difficult relationships and situations.

In the next essay under "Vision and Principles," entitled "Receiving Gifts in Ecumenical Dialogue," Margaret O'Gara further explains how ecumenical research fits teaching and working in the mode of witness, particularly witnessing to the full unity of the church. She points out that when people work together in an ecumenical context, they may affirm "alternate formulations of the commonly confessed faith," bring together "complementary points that were once considered contradictory," and "exchange very different gifts through dialogue."[93] These actions are supported by a stance of repentance that helps the participants discern "whether it is divisive sectarianism or love for Gospel truth which leads them to reject a position offered to them as a gift by a partner church."[94] It takes time to do so, time for personal examination as well as intellectual questioning. Working from a common faith in Jesus Christ, those engaging in ecumenical research through the lens of receptive ecumenism can foster their willingness to listen to other scholars with viewpoints very different from their own not just for a day or a week but for years. Doing so is its own spiritual discipline, an action of the heart as much as an action of the intellect. Such

---

92. Ibid., 17.
93. O'Gara, "Receiving Gifts," 29.
94. Ibid., 31.

research "calls for willingness to enter into relationships, to risk vulnerability for the sake of the common effort, and to refuse competition as an acceptable model for serious inquiry."[95] This model certainly fits into the scheme of communion ecclesiology explicitly embodied in the graduate theology curriculum of Mount Angel Seminary, as well as implicitly within its undergraduate curriculum of philosophy and the humanities. The best teaching, the best research, occurs when a larger project or purpose is at the center of our endeavors. Thus receptive ecumenism offers an alternative mode to more competitive forms of scholarship by "recalling scholars to an earlier ideal of being truly a college together. In such a context, reception becomes possible."[96] Receptive ecumenism does not eschew vigor; it does eschew, however, competitiveness of the sort that leads to distortion of the truth rather than a fuller understanding or expression of it.

The context of receptive ecumenism makes additional demands on my commitment to learning from Orthodoxy through my study of iconography and the various ways in which I have taught and offered it to others, including Catholic seminary students. It should move forward in the years to come as a serious academic and spiritual commitment rather than just for the duration of a particular class, presentation, or the week or so of the year that I attend the Iconographic Arts Institute. However, even for simple logistical reasons, working from my home tradition of Catholicism and seeking to engage with the Orthodox tradition is a challenge. For instance, compared to the number of Catholics in the United States, the numbers of Orthodox are small, so visiting an Orthodox Church is not an easy task. The closest Orthodox community to my home is a mission, so it does not have a full schedule of services, though I have attended some of them, as well as some sessions on an introduction to Orthodoxy that they have offered. Much can be learned from our own study, and fortunately more and higher quality information about Orthodoxy is being made available to the general public, yet this does not replace the lived experience of Orthodox liturgies and an Orthodox spirituality and way of life with all of its challenges and joys. Additionally, at this point of my ministry, a path to full-time study of iconography has not been a possibility. Overall, because receptive ecumenism includes honoring our current situation, I find this approach fits my circumstances well, and it is possible that others may find it fruitful because of their own professional and personal commitments.

95. Ibid., 33.
96. Ibid.

One essay in *Receptive Ecumenism and the Catholic Call to Learning* is written from an Orthodox point of view and highlights some of the challenges that come with approaching Orthodoxy from another Christian community. In the opening of his essay entitled "Receptive Ecumenism and Catholic Learning—an Orthodox Perspective," Andrew Louth affirms that while the project to which the volume is dedicated focuses on Roman Catholics learning from other Christian communities, "we are all clear, I think, that the process of listening—critical and reflective listening—must always be a two-way process."[97] Having said this, he explains some of the challenges for those seeking to learn from Orthodoxy. He begins by stating that Orthodoxy understands itself as "a seamless unity of faith, worship, and practice" and that "the very essence of Orthodoxy is an immersion in a way of life."[98] He points out, and as many students of Orthodoxy have experienced, Orthodox theology is not easily summarized; it is better prayed and sung. A person must get inside the prayers, inside the singing, in order to truly and deeply learn from Orthodoxy. Louth uses the example of the role of the spiritual father in the Orthodox tradition to explain this point. Accepting the guidance of a spiritual father means accepting a way of life in which "one does not choose what to listen to from one's spiritual father."[99] As with the Orthodox tradition as a whole, every aspect of the relationship, those parts that seem easier as well as those parts that are more challenging or intimidating, need to be lived in some way if a person is to take part in the relationship, in the tradition, in its fullness.

In response to another essay in *Receptive Ecumenism and the Call to Catholic Learning*, Louth also discusses how eucharistic ecclesiology is lived out in the Orthodox Church. The essay to which he is responding is "Catholic Learning and Orthodoxy—the Promise and Challenge of Eucharistic Ecclesiology," by Paul McPartlan. Louth carefully explains that he supports the process of receptive ecumenism and does not intend his remarks to be critical of McPartlan. Rather, he points out that his remarks are more self-critical toward Orthodoxy than toward the learning process in which those taking part in receptive ecumenism are engaged. He explains that "there is a real danger when reading Metropolitan John [Zizioulas], or appreciative expositions of this thought, of being lulled into a sense that

---

97. Louth, "Receptive Ecumenism," 361.
98. Ibid.
99. Ibid., 362.

this is how we Orthodox live our ecclesiology."¹⁰⁰ Essentially, Louth is offering appropriate advice to those who wish, and rightly so, to learn from Orthodox theology. Louth cautions Catholics and other Christians against idealizing Orthodoxy to the extent that their understanding of Orthodoxy becomes inaccurate or unrealistic.

First, he points out that while eucharistic ecclesiology is certainly fundamental in Orthodoxy, "it was not until the last century that this eucharistic ecclesiology found explicit theological expression."¹⁰¹ A renewed sense of eucharistic ecclesiology came through the focus on patristic scholarship on the part of Catholics and other Christian scholars who made more texts and translations available to the scholarly community, which was a gift to many, including the Orthodox. Thus, according to Louth, the Orthodox were more the receivers than the originators of this gift, making it "an example of Receptive Ecumenism" on their part rather than the other way around.¹⁰²

Second, Louth asks his audience to acknowledge that the rhetoric surrounding communion in the Orthodox Church is not always met by the reality on the ground. For instance, outside of Orthodox countries such as Greece and Russia, overlapping jurisdictions violate the ideal of having one bishop in a particular major location around whom all of the faithful of that area gather. In many places in the diaspora, communities are organized into exarchates that contain an archbishop who is appointed by a patriarch, thus preventing the archbishop in question from having any episcopal independence. Concerning the structure of the episcopacy, he writes, "Not only is there little trace of any kind of 'eucharistic' ecclesiology, there is often enough little trace of the *communio* or *koinonia*, that [McPartlan] remarked on as characteristic of the ecclesiology of the first millennium and still of the Orthodox."¹⁰³ Louth also points out that eucharistic ecclesiology implies a sense of good communication among the patriarchates, yet even this is often missing.¹⁰⁴ Concerning institutional structures, he explains that some Orthodox writers tend to degrade the institutional model of the

---

100. Ibid.
101. Ibid., 364.
102. Ibid., 365.
103. Ibid., 366.
104. Ibid.

church in favor of a more mystical view, and such writers fail to realize the necessity of those institutional structures.[105]

In the last section of his essay, Louth discusses the ecclesiology explored by a number of Orthodox theologians, an ecclesiology that "all Orthodox theologians would want to embrace."[106] This ecclesiology is based in mutuality among bishops, between the bishop and the synod, between the local and the universal. However, Louth asks "that we attend to what happens, and not just to theory. Orthodox are just as good as Catholics at paying synodality little more than lip service."[107] He points out that portions of the Orthodox world, particularly Romania, actually have a synodal system that works, yet other parts of the world do not. He uses his experience of his own Russian Orthodox diocese to point out how the lack of such a system actually led to a split in his diocese. As good and desirable as synodality is, Louth wants his readers to remember that his own experience shows that "Orthodox ecclesiology is not all that it seems!"[108] Essentially, Louth sees receptive ecumenism as a worthy project for Catholics and Orthodox alike. At the same time, we must heed the actual situations in which our ecclesiology is lived rather than just the theory that lies behind it. Catholic seminary students and all students of iconography can apply a similar lesson to their studies as well. We certainly can and should learn all we can about the canon and tradition of iconography. At the same time, that isn't enough. We need to pay attention to how the icon is used, well and poorly, by actual people, and how our studies affect our own practices as well as those of our families, parishes, and communities.

At this point, further discussion of one of the main points that separates the Roman Catholic Church and the Orthodox Church, papal primacy, may be helpful. Many books and other publications have been written on the subject from both the Roman Catholic and Orthodox perspectives, and navigating through all of that material is challenging at best for those who are studying iconography and wish to understand this important issue. A recent book by Laurent A. Cleenewerck, *His Broken Body: Understanding and Healing the Schism between the Roman Catholic and Eastern Orthodox Churches*, may be of help in this regard. Cleenewerck wrote this book in order to provide a clear and balanced discussion of papal primacy, the kind

---

105. Ibid.
106. Ibid., 368.
107. Ibid.
108. Ibid., 369.

of discussion that he found lacking in many of the materials, both popular and scholarly, offered by both Catholics and the Orthodox. His work gives the clearest presentation of papal primacy that I have found thus far, and he discusses the other issues that contribute to the divisions between East and West as well. Perhaps the discussion that is presented here will urge readers to work with Cleenewerck's book in its entirety. The purpose of this discussion is not polemical; it is an effort to assist those who encounter the issue of papal primacy during their study of iconography, as they inevitably will, to gain more clarity about this question.

Cleenewerck focuses on ecclesiology as the main division between the Roman Catholic Church and the Eastern Orthodox Church. He explains that "a different understanding of Petrine succession and 'universal' ecclesiology is at the root of the separation between East and West," a difference that began as early as the second century.[109] Throughout his book, he argues that the understanding of the church living undivided during the first Christian millennium is not entirely accurate; rather, "at best . . . (local) Churches within the Roman Empire were in communion with each other most of the time, albeit with significant periods of external 'disunity.'"[110] This is important because often the study of iconography in an ecumenical setting is based on the understanding that we are drawing on a common tradition from a time in church history during which the Christian world was one. The common tradition is certainly true, but we don't want to create a utopian version of church history that does not stand up to scrutiny. As with all students of theology and church history, regardless of the specific discipline with which they are engaged, Catholic seminarians and iconographers need a realistic understanding of their tradition. Cleenewerck explains that the divide between East and West grew as two different ecclesiologies continued to develop, and he concludes that if the issue of primacy is to be resolved, the 34th apostolic canon and the Council of Sardica provide the best route to unity between East and West.[111]

Before returning to the issue of primacy, a short overview of the rest of Cleenewerck's book is helpful. In his first section, he covers the common ground shared by the Roman Catholic Church and the Eastern Orthodox Church, including the creed, the apostolic tradition, and apostolic succession. Both churches, he explains, have in common the following: (1) an

---

109. Cleenewerck, *His Broken Body*, 31.
110. Ibid.
111. Ibid.

understanding of the apostolic tradition as "something distinct from (and coherent with) the canonical New Testament," (2) apostolic succession that is manifested in the order of deacon, presbyter, and bishop, (3) the understanding of sacrament or mystery, (4) the baptism of infants, (5) an understanding of the Eucharist as a sacrifice, (6) reception of the Old Testament, (7) prayer for the dead, (8) veneration of saints and a variety of holy objects, (9) liturgical worship, and (10) the perpetual virginity of the Mother of God.[112]

In his first section, he also outlines the major and minor differences between the Roman Catholic Church and the Eastern Orthodox Church that he discusses more in depth for the rest of his book. While different issues have been given more emphasis at different points in history, he offers the following list: (1) the *filioque* clause in the creed, (2) the role of the papacy as defined by the Catholic Church at Vatican I, (3) presbyteral celibacy, (4) annulments and divorce, (5) the use of leavened bread, (6) the priest facing the people, (7) the practice of beards, (8) the use of altar girls, (9) the "absence" of epiclesis in the Roman Mass, (10) the doctrine of purgatory and indulgences, (11) the Augustinian views of original sin, (12) the Roman Catholic Marian dogmas of 1854 and 1950, and (13) variations in devotional practices, such as eucharistic adoration and celebration of the Sacred Heart.[113]

Cleenewerck makes papal primacy the primary though not exclusive focus of the rest of his book. After his first section, he devotes the second section to the ecclesiology that developed in both the East and the West. Section 3 offers a historical perspective on the ongoing tension between unity and disunity, including the councils, schisms, and writings of the fathers that pertain to that tension, and section 4 offers the theological perspective of the Roman Catholic Church, the Eastern Orthodox Church, as well as material from the church fathers. Section 5 discusses differences other than ecclesiology and the papacy, and in the final section Cleenewerck offers a model and vision for unity that could come to pass between the Roman Catholic Church and the Eastern Orthodox Church.

Since the audience for this book is primarily Catholic seminarians and students of the icon, who are more likely to be more familiar with Catholicism than with Eastern Orthodoxy, the short discussion of primacy below will focus more on the understanding of primacy from the point of view

112. Ibid., 51.
113. Ibid., 55.

of the Orthodox. At the beginning of his section on ecclesiology, Cleenewerck explains that "the Church, strictly speaking is the Body of Christ, the eschatological reality of all those who have been united to Christ's life in all times and all places."[114] This corresponds to Dulles's model of the church as a mystical communion. Additionally, he explains that the church also refers to "the gathering of Christians in a given area to celebrate the Eucharist."[115] Where the Eucharist is properly celebrated, the church is present. This certainly resonates with the phrase in Catholic theology that originated with Henri de Lubac that the Eucharist makes the Church.

Cleenewerck's next point works with the difference of understanding or emphasis between the Roman Catholic Church and the Eastern Orthodox Church regarding papal primacy. Cleenewerck argues that an understanding of a universal church should refer to the eschatological nature of the Church rather than a worldwide visible society, a body in which each part is a complete whole capable of standing on its own, like a hologram.[116] Essentially, it is in the relationship of the parts to the whole that the difference between the ecclesiology of the Roman Catholic Church and the Eastern Orthodox Church comes into sharper relief. Does each part, each individual place where the Eucharist is celebrated, need to have a binding, institutional relationship with another particular part of the whole in order to be considered part of the church? Does each part need that relationship with the pope, the bishop of Rome? This is the difference as explained by Cleenewerck: "Where the Orthodox would say that every (local) Church has a universal, missionary vocation, Roman Catholics tend to see universality or internationalism as an ontological requirement from the start."[117] Therefore, as Cleenewerck states at the end of his section on the structure of the Catholic Church, any local or particular church "seems to exist as a manifestation of the universal (worldwide) Church."[118] Therefore, a local church can only be "catholic," if it is in communion with Rome, and even then it is still only a part of the whole rather than containing all that is essential to be whole, to be fully the Church, on its own.

Building on this essential difference in their understanding of ecclesiology and the place that it gives to the bishop of Rome, Cleenewerck

---

114. Ibid., 63.
115. Ibid.
116. Ibid., 68–69.
117. Ibid., 70.
118. Ibid., 95.

summarizes the ways in which the Eastern Orthodox understanding of primacy differs from that of the Roman Catholic Church in seven points. First, Orthodoxy acknowledges the ministries of bishop, priest, and deacon, and even when a bishop is recognized with an additional title, he remains a peer of his brother bishops. According to Cleenewerck's explanation, Roman Catholicism holds that the pope holds an office above that of bishop by which he holds episcopal powers that the other bishops do not, essentially making him a bishop of bishops.[119] Roman Catholics would not necessarily accept this explanation. In a strict theological sense, the pope, the bishop of Rome, has the same episcopal powers as the rest of his brother bishops. He has juridical authority that the other bishops do not, but this should not be confused with episcopal authority.

Cleenewerck's second point on the understanding of primacy from the point of view of the Orthodox is tied to the first: any primacy exercised by the bishop of Rome must be done with the common consent of the other bishops. Third, rather than the bishop of Rome holding the ultimate authority in the Church, an ecumenical council holds the ultimate authority. From the point of view of the Eastern Orthodox Church, it seems inconsistent that it was due to a declaration made by the First Vatican Council that the Roman Catholic Church defined that the pope does not need a council to decide matters of faith and morals.[120] When it comes to the actual term "primacy," for the Eastern Orthodox Church it is "more a matter of canonical procedure and Church administration than a matter of faith."[121] Cleenewerck then builds his last three points, which all concern Peter, on this definition of primacy with a focus on church administration.

First, the ecclesiology of the Eastern Orthodox understands that every bishop holds the place of Peter within his particular, local church.[122] As we will see in his outline of the steps that could move the Roman Catholic Church and the Eastern Orthodox Church toward greater unity, the 34th canon of the Council of Sardica of 344 has a key place for Cleenewerck. The canon is worth quoting in full:

> It behooves the Bishops of every nation to know the one among them who is the premier or chief, and to recognize him as their head, and to refrain from doing anything superfluous without his

---

119. Ibid., 117.
120. Ibid., 118.
121. Ibid.
122. Ibid.

advice and approval: but, instead, each of them should do only whatever is necessitated by his own parish and by the territories under him. But let not even such a one do anything without the advice and consent and approval of all. For this will there be concord, and God will be glorified through the Lord in the Holy Spirit, the Father, and the Son, and the Holy Spirit.[123]

Through a reading of this canon, Cleenewerck understands that the place of Peter and the responsibilities to the faithful in a given area which that place entails are not restricted to the bishop of Rome. Additionally, the Orthodox understand that any primacy that Peter did hold in relationship to the other apostles was that of being "first among the twelve, not over them."[124] In this way, primacy was exercised with the other apostles rather than separate from the rest of the apostles. Lastly, Cleenewerck points out that in terms of geography, Peter left successors in Rome, Alexandria, and Antioch. In this way, Alexandria and Antioch would share a similar historical honor as that of Rome. However, Cleenewerck points out that "in the Eastern mind, it does not follow that these bishops are more 'successors of Peter' than other bishops—what matters is biblical and patristic ecclesiology, not historical pedigrees."[125] Therefore, the bishops of all three patriarchates, including the bishop of Rome, would not hold any additional primacy over the bishops of the other patriarchates or any of the other bishops throughout the world.

This canon was also used for support in the document issued in September of 2016 by the Joint International Commission for Theological Dialogue between the Roman Catholic Church and the Orthodox Church. The document, entitled "Synodality and Primacy during the First Millennium: Towards a Common Understanding in Service to the Unity of the Church," includes the canon in its third section, entitled "The Regional Communion of Churches." The document states that it "offers a canonical description of the correlation between the protos [the first among the bishops of a region] and the other bishops of each region."[126] While this dialogue may not be at the point Cleenewerck suggests of making more explicit use of this canon as a way toward more structural unity, it is heartening to see it included in the common heritage between the Roman Catholic Church and the Orthodox Church that may help these two bodies grow together into the future.

---

123. Cummings, *Rudder*, 50.
124. Cleenewerck, *His Broken Body*, 118.
125. Ibid., 119.
126. Joint International Commission, "Synodality and Primacy," para. 13.

In the conclusion of his book, Cleenewerck offers his vision for a way forward for unity between the Roman Catholic Church and the Eastern Orthodox Church. He admits that unity is not likely to happen in the near future, and that in some respects, both churches lack a model on which to build such unity. According to Cleenewerck, this is because "we have retained the language of early Christianity: deacons, presbyters, bishops, tradition, etc, but the meaning of these words has profoundly changed" throughout Christian history.[127] We no longer follow the model of a bishop, presbyters, and deacons in each town or city. Cleenewerck suggests returning to a more truly apostolic model of ecclesiology in both the East and the West. Perhaps in doing so, more Catholics and Orthodox would more easily connect with the institutional structures of the church and find them more meaningful.

Cleenewerck argues that to move forward Catholics must become Orthodox in some respects, and the Orthodox must become Catholic in some respects. For their part, he explains, Catholics need to rediscover and embrace "the liturgical spirit of Eastern Christianity," which would naturally lead to "the embracing of eschatological-Eucharistic ecclesiology and pre-Nicene theology."[128] He argues that giving more emphasis to an understanding of the liturgy as a heavenly liturgy would help prepare the Roman Catholic Church for a reconciliation with the Eastern Orthodox Church. On the part of the Orthodox, they need to recognize the need for a worldwide structure that can address the "catholic-universal nature of the Church."[129] Cleenewerck points out that "the ability of the Church of Rome to coordinate worldwide mission, social work and a consistent doctrinal message should make the Orthodox think," and such centrality and coordination need not be yoked with complete infallibility.[130] Lastly, Cleenewerck reiterates his point about a return to Sardica and how the pertinent canon provides the best way to enable both the Roman Catholic Church and the Eastern Orthodox Church to move forward as well as closer to one another.

Cleenewerck includes an appendix in his book entitled "The Unity Process," which gives a succinct outline of the preliminary work that he thinks needs to be done by both the Roman Catholic Church and the Orthodox Church if unity is to be achieved, even if that unity occurs well into

---

127. Cleenewerck, *His Broken Body*, 424.
128. Ibid., 426.
129. Ibid., 427.
130. Ibid.

the future. It may be helpful for readers to keep this material in mind as they move into the next section on the Orthodox and ecumenism. For the Roman Catholics, Cleenewerck outlines the following steps: (1) returning to the model of heavenly liturgics, (2) adopting a eucharistic ecclesiology, which does not necessarily discount the need for a worldwide institutional structure, (3) more patristic-based curriculum in seminaries, and (4) the publication of preconciliar documents prior to a future council that would focus on unity between the Roman Catholic Church and the Eastern Orthodox Church. For the Eastern Orthodox, Cleenewerck outlines the following: (1) creating a pan-Orthodox organizational structure, (2) publishing a common catechism, (3) engaging in liturgical renewal through the patristic tradition, and (4) the publication of preconciliar documents. Overall, Cleenewerck's list offers us a simple though not simplistic understanding of how the conversation between the Roman Catholic Church and the Eastern Orthodox Church could move into the future. Much serious and soul-searching work is needed, as is indicated by the steps he lists before the publication of preconciliar documents, yet the fruit of such work could also be immense and would certainly touch the work and lives of those with an interest in and devotion to the icon.

Orthodoxy and Ecumenism

Receptive ecumenism encourages openness, but that does not necessarily mean that openness will be reciprocated in the same way in which we offer it to other Christians and their traditions. In this section, three additional authors and documents help us understand how the Orthodox view and participate in ecumenism, and this understanding can help lessen the number of misunderstandings that may arise as the non-Orthodox, particularly seminarians interested in iconography and those in training as iconographers, pursue receptive ecumenism and the call to Catholic learning in relation to the Orthodox tradition.

In his well-known and well-respected book, *The Orthodox Church*, Timothy Ware gives one of the clearest explanations that I have found of the approach of the Orthodox Church to ecumenism and the place the Orthodox hold within the ecumenical movement. He explains that the Orthodox Church "in all humility . . . believes itself to be the 'one, holy, Catholic and Apostolic Church,' of which the Creed speaks," a belief that guides all of their relations with other Christians.[131] They hold that what the Orthodox celebrate, explore and defend through their theological work is that which was handed down by the earliest Christians and is consistent with that early faith. Adherence to that faith assures them that Orthodox Christianity is the most authentic expression of Christianity. Given this starting point, it is logical that Ware would explain that this understanding leads to the conclusion that the goal of ecumenical work is the "reconciliation of all Christians to Orthodoxy."[132] Essentially, Ware explains, non-Orthodox Christians should understand that statements such as this come from a place of love and respect for the faith rather than a desire to exclude anyone from that faith.

Ware also explains that the Orthodox world is not any more monolithic than the Catholic or larger Christian world; within Orthodoxy, different groups take different stances toward ecumenism. While those who study Orthodoxy should certainly take these different views into account, we should not mistakenly think one part represents the whole when it does not. "Although nearly all Orthodox are agreed in their fundamental teaching concerning the Church," explains Ware, "they do not entirely agree concerning the practical consequences which follow from this teaching."[133] Where different groups of Orthodox fall on this question seems to correspond to which model of the church they may hold.

The more moderate group, explains Ware, does not hold that people who are not Orthodox do not belong to the Church in any way. Because the Spirit blows where it will and because where the Spirit exists the Church exists, "invisible bonds may exist despite an outward separation."[134] This corresponds to the model of the church as a mystical communion and prevents those who hold this view from passing judgment on non-Orthodox Christians. The ways in which non-Orthodox Christians differ from the Orthodox varies greatly; some are very close to Orthodoxy while others are not. According to this point of view, this variety of belief among the non-Orthodox needs to be taken into account, and non-Orthodox Christians should not be regarded in the same way as nonbelievers.[135]

131. Ware, *Orthodox Church*, 307.
132. Ibid., 309.
133. Ibid., 308.
134. Ibid.
135. Ibid., 309.

Additionally, Ware points out that structurally, the desire to bring all Christians to Orthodoxy should not be confused with a desire to make other Christians subject to a particular jurisdiction. Should more structural unity be established between the Orthodox and other Christian communities, those communities would be made a part of Orthodoxy's own decentralized structure without losing their autonomy. For the Orthodox, unity among Christians requires a unity of faith from which would flow a unity in the sacraments. However, even those two requirements leave much space for the variety of human and Christian experience and expression. The Orthodox and the Christians who may be united with them could still have room for "many different cultural patterns, for many different ways of worship, and even for many different systems of outward organization."[136] Overall, Ware's point here can keep Catholics and other Christians from projecting onto the Orthodox a rigidity that is not an accurate reflection of their point of view toward ecumenism.

The second group holds a stricter point of view. Catholic seminarians and other students of iconography, Orthodoxy, and ecumenism who speak or work with those from this point of view "should not forget that such opinions are held today by Orthodox of great holiness and loving compassion."[137] Those with this point of view believe that the church cannot be split or lose its essential unity; therefore, anyone who is separated from the church for any reason ceases to be a member of the church. They affirm that the non-Orthodox can certainly love God and receive God's mercy, but that does not mean it is appropriate to call them members of the Orthodox Church.

Ware also carefully explains the issues that separate the Orthodox from other Christian communities, including the Roman Catholic Church. He discusses the great amount of common ground shared by the Orthodox and Roman Catholics, as well as the basic doctrinal, canonical, and cultural issues that contribute to the separation between the two. The key issue is the role of the pope, since the Orthodox do not accept the definition from the First Vatican Council concerning the pope's infallibility and universal jurisdiction. Ware explains that the Orthodox are open to an understanding of the Petrine ministry that grants the pope "an all-embracing apostolic care . . . and not only [the right to] accept appeals from the whole Christian world, but even to take the initiative in seeking ways of healing when crisis

---

136. Ibid., 310.
137. Ibid., 309.

and conflict arise anywhere among Christians."[138] Essentially, his ministry would be pastoral rather than juridical.

The Orthodox, Ware also claims, are in a unique position to help other Western Christians who are authentically searching for a doctrinally sound and historically based Christian faith. Orthodoxy lives outside of an important set of ideas that has influenced Western Christianity since it "has undergone no scholastic revolution, no Reformation and Counter-Reformation, but still lives in that older Tradition of the Fathers which so many in the west now desire to recover."[139] The Orthodox can question this experience in the West and "offer a middle path between fundamentalist literalism and the semi-agnosticism of the extreme liberals."[140] Both the East and the West have much to learn and offer to the other, all for the sake of a deeper and more transforming discipleship in Jesus Christ.

Through several essays in his book *Speaking the Truth in Love: Education, Mission, and Witness in Contemporary Orthodoxy*, Father Thomas Hopko also helps us to understand the resistance to ecumenism that is within Orthodox communities today. In the West, much of this resistance has come from Christians who joined Orthodoxy from other Christian communities. It also comes from some Orthodox monasteries that identify everything that deviates in any way from Orthodox practice and belief as heretical and dangerous. According to Hopko, "they see no possibility for these Christian communities to make common confessions of faith with the Orthodox."[141] Overall, those who take this point of view think any participation in ecumenical work, by its very nature, would require them to deny that the Orthodox Church is the one, holy, catholic, and apostolic Church. This most critical attack states that the very act of participating in the ecumenical movement in any way is heretical. While it is more likely that Catholic seminarians and students of iconography will encounter this point of view more in their reading than through personal contact, it is still important to understand it exists and to not be discouraged or intimidated by it.[142] As receptive ecumenism explains, students can learn about and from Orthodoxy even if these parts of the Orthodox world do not want to reciprocate.

---

138. Ibid., 316.
139. Ibid., 325.
140. Ibid., 326.
141. Hopko, *Speaking the Truth in Love*, 146.
142. Ibid., 147.

Despite the vigor of these objections, Hopko explains that "the condemnation of ecumenism, and its identification as apostasy and heresy, is something new in the Orthodox Church."[143] Other new teachings that are often found alongside the condemnation of ecumenism include the nonexistence of sacramental grace outside of the Orthodox Church, the rebaptizing of Christians from other communities who become Orthodox, and the understanding of every piece of Orthodox teaching and tradition, big and small, as absolutely essential. Hopko explains that with this point of view, questioning anything within Orthodoxy "renders one unfaithful to Orthodoxy."[144] He also explains that these teachings are not found in the Bible or among the church fathers and saints until very recently, and even some of those, while urging the Orthodox to avoid unbelievers, "went among them to try to win them to God."[145] Thus, overall, while it is helpful to be aware of these objections to the whole project of ecumenism among some of the Orthodox, we should also keep in mind the larger context for those objections which Hopko offers.

Along with the objections above, he explains some criticisms of ecumenism that are offered by the Orthodox who have actually been involved in ecumenical work. Hopko goes so far as to say that such criticisms have been "so constant and consistent since the beginning of Orthodox involvement in ecumenism, they could be considered a customary and essential aspect of the work."[146] We should keep in mind that criticism, in and of itself, does not need to be considered negative or condemnatory. Criticism can help to clarify the thinking involved in ecumenism. Hopko points out that while the critics of Orthodox participation in ecumenical work have commented on meetings and gatherings, official reports and documents, and the quality of the participants, they have never condemned the participation itself.

Orthodox critics have especially focused on the common worship offered during ecumenical gatherings, but they have not said common worship in and of itself, when done with the proper guidance and boundaries, is sinful. They have also recognized that at times the Orthodox Church has not had the resources to properly participate in ecumenical work or gatherings, thus making their participation more of a hindrance than a benefit. Overall,

143. Ibid., 148.
144. Ibid., 149.
145. Ibid.
146. Ibid., 149–50.

these critics "defended proper and competent Orthodox participation in ecumenical work" and understand their criticism to be pointing out the times when the quality of the participation was detrimental to Orthodoxy and ecumenism.[147] When it is carried out with the proper care and preparation, the participation of the Orthodox in ecumenical work supports their Christian mission and their witness to Christ. Hopko argues that despite the negative views of ecumenism among some of the Orthodox, ecumenical work provides a "unique opportunity to witness to Christ," to love one's enemies, and to meet non-Orthodox Christians who "for all the errors and mistakes of their respective churches, can be real disciples of Jesus Christ."[148] Lastly, participation in ecumenical activities pushes the Orthodox to understand themselves more fully, including the discrepancies between words spoken and lives lived which concerns Andrew Louth.

Hopko concludes that while discernment is needed to decide which ecumenical activities to take part in, and while some Orthodox churches have legitimate reasons for not participating in ecumenical activities, ecumenism is still a duty for those who have discerned well and can participate. Generally speaking, Orthodox Christians are "obliged to work in whatever ways the Lord provides to meet and cooperate with non-Orthodox Christians, and indeed all people, for the sake of whatever is true, honorable, just, pure, lovely, gracious, excellent, and worthy of praise (Phil. 4.8)."[149] Let us hope that work with and through the icon may be counted among those areas of study and action that may be counted as worthy of praise, for the Orthodox and non-Orthodox alike.

Lastly, a document composed in 1973 by the Standing Conference of the Canonical Orthodox Bishops in the Americas entitled *Guidelines for Orthodox Christians in Ecumenical Relations* offers more practical details concerning relations between Orthodox and the non-Orthodox, similar to the *Directory for the Application of Principles and Norms of Ecumenism* from the Roman Catholic Church. The ecumenical movement, states the introduction, "is an expression of love and hope in an otherwise bewildered and tired world order."[150] Thus, as Hopko points out, the purpose of Orthodox participation in ecumenism and thus these guidelines is to help the Orthodox provide a solid witness to other Christians and all

---

147. Ibid., 150.
148. Ibid., 158.
149. Ibid., 160.
150 Stephanopoulos, "Guidelines."

of humanity. In his introduction to the document, Archbishop Iakovos explains that it offers a "consistent ecumenical policy, based upon the ecclesiological and evangelical doctrines of the Orthodox faith."[151] In addition to guidelines specifically for the clergy, the guidelines include general principles of Orthodox ecumenism and a collection of statements made by Orthodox clergy in the twentieth century that provide the basis for an Orthodox ecumenical policy. A reading of this document can help Catholic seminarians and all students of the icon and of Orthodoxy understand some necessary details involved with learning from the Orthodox tradition on an experiential basis.

The first section of part 1 of the guidelines acknowledges the limited participation the Orthodox had in the ecumenical movement up until 1973. However, certain basic principles have been developed, particularly beginning with the Patriarchal and Synodal Encyclical of 1920. These principles emphasize that "the ecumenical problem for us is the problem of the disunity of Christendom and the necessity of the recovery of the biblical-patristic synthesis of faith which is constitutive of the one Church."[152] The guidelines are not intended to be "a final statement on the matter of Orthodox ecumenical relations" but to give more consistency to ecumenical practices among the Orthodox in the United States.[153]

The guidelines go on to explain two basic ecumenical principles for the Orthodox, the Confessional principle and the Ecclesiological principle.[154] The Confessional principle states that the apostolic tradition is the basis for Christian unity, and while disunity many be influenced by historical and cultural factors, divisions are "ultimately rooted in deviations from the one faith."[155] Compromise in its negative sense of improperly diminishing the truth of the faith should not be a strategy for healing those divisions. Rather, the study of issues in the light of "the very sources of Revelation" should be the guiding strategy and principle as the Orthodox pursue greater unity with other Christians.[156] Second, the Ecclesiological principle states that the goal of the ecumenical movement is the unity of humanity in the one Church and that the "Orthodox Church is the visible,

---

151. Ibid.
152. Ibid., 2.
153. Ibid., 4.
154. Ibid., 3.
155. Ibid.
156. Ibid.

historical realization of the one Church."[157] Other concerns or principles, whether they are social, political, or secular, cannot take the place of the Church serving as the organizing principle for ecumenical work. Thus, according to the guidelines, the only goal worth holding in the ecumenical movement is that of realizing a true Christian community that is rooted in the Orthodox Church.

Next, the guidelines explain several other principles that, along with the Confessional and Ecclesiological principles, "underlie and hopefully illuminate the practical suggestions contained in these Guidelines."[158] These principles include that Christ founded one true Church on the apostles rather than many churches, and that the true Church is "visibly present in the historical Orthodox community."[159] All members of the Church are to pray for Christian unity and take every action available to them to encourage that unity. When engaging in ecumenical work, the truth must be spoken in love without compromising Orthodox teaching and with respect regarding the sincerity of the convictions of others. Thus, as the guidelines point out, the work of clear communication "in love and truth is basic to the ecumenical task."[160] This means that the Orthodox must understand and study their own tradition and live it out as best as they can in order to be the best witnesses to the faith as they can. That learning is supported by an awareness of more utopian tendencies that can be found among some from various Christian communities who pursue ecumenical work, tendencies that amount to false teachings. They are at the opposite end of the spectrum of those Orthodox who find all ecumenical work heretical. Overall, these two principles coincide with the principles of Catholic ecumenism as well, the principles of knowing our own tradition and communicating it clearly and with respect for the integrity of the tradition.

In the section entitled "Orthodox Ecumenical Witness," the guidelines point out several other elements of that witness. "The principle of autocephaly is fundamental to Orthodox ecclesiology," and this includes the structure of the universal episcopate, ecumenical councils, and the work of the Ecumenical Patriarch of Constantinople.[161] In support of this principle, "intra-Orthodox jurisdictional relations must be maintained"

157. Ibid.
158. Ibid.
159. Ibid.
160. Ibid., 4.
161. Ibid., 5.

and respected, and the work of the Standing Conference of Orthodox Bishops in America, the originators of the guidelines, should be supported by the faithful as well.[162] Along with the clergy, the faithful can develop appropriate ecumenical sensibilities in the home, in schools, and through various programs of religious education. The clergy are encouraged to offer education and materials about ecumenism in their community and to offer appropriate input to other Christians who inquire about Orthodoxy. "No opportunity," explain the guidelines, "should be avoided to contribute to the knowledge of the precious heritage of Orthodoxy."[163] Given this, those who study and teach iconography should take advantage of every opportunity that presents itself to learn from the clergy and other Orthodox who offer such programs, as well as to seek them out as presenters for their own programs and workshops when appropriate.

A significant portion of the rest of the guidelines gives directives primarily for the conduct of Orthodox clergy. For Catholic seminarians and other students of iconography and Orthodoxy, this portion can help them understand the responses and behaviors they might encounter when they visit an Orthodox parish, particularly if it is over an extended period of time. For instance, a section is dedicated to worship with non-Orthodox Christians. This section explains that the Orthodox Church clearly differentiates between liturgical and non-liturgical prayer, a distinction that Roman Catholics ought to easily recognize as well. Non-liturgical prayer is "to be prudently used within the context of the ecumenical movement and the pluralistic setting of our society."[164] Because liturgical prayer, the celebration of the Eucharist and the reception of Communion, is the fulfillment of Christian unity, it is offered only to members of the Orthodox Church; the sacrament "must not be understood or implemented as means toward that unity."[165] This stance ought to be familiar to Roman Catholics, given that the Roman Catholic Church does not normally open communion to non-Catholics other than the Orthodox. The guidelines explain that while non-Orthodox may certainly be invited to attend Orthodox services so as to learn about the Orthodox spiritual heritage, it should be made clear to the guests that a deeper sacramental communion is not "intended or

162. Ibid.
163. Ibid., 6.
164. Ibid., 11.
165. Ibid.

implied by such attendance."[166] If our studies proceed in such a way that we grow in love for the iconographic and Orthodox tradition, such separation may be painful, but perhaps that is as it should be and can urge us to further ecumenical work and deeper prayer for us all.

The last portion of the section on Orthodoxy and ecumenism is dedicated to one specific consideration of the connection between ecumenism and the icon developed by Father Steven Bigham, an Orthodox priest, university professor, and a well-known author of books on iconography. He has published a six-part series of articles on *Orthodox Arts Journal*, an online journal that publishes material from many of the best iconographers and scholars of the icon today. His series is entitled "The Icon: Sign of Unity or Division?," and he considers the role, if any, Christian art has in keeping Christians divided from one another or moving them toward greater unity. He points out that in our own time the subject of iconoclasm, idolatry, and the role of Christian art "has nearly disappeared from intra-Christian discussions."[167] Nevertheless, he concludes that because the icon and ecumenism are in and of themselves prominent though often separate in discussions today, it is useful to consider how they speak to one another as well.

Bigham first considers the points that almost all Christians can affirm about Christian images. He discusses how Christians today would approach the arguments that were made by opponents of the icon during the iconoclastic movement. Bigham explains that if any Christian today tried to assert that any image of Jesus is by its very nature idolatrous, "that person's opinion would be universally rejected."[168] Images of Jesus appear everywhere in churches and publications across the Christian world. Second, he points out that no Christians today truly conflate the substances of the type and prototype of an image. "It seems so obvious, what the council [Nicaea II] decided," explains Bigham, that "an image and the person represented are of two different substances, but they are linked by likeness."[169] Nor would many if any Christians assert that we dishonor Christ and his saints by representing them in matter through an image because they think matter is too vulgar.

---

166. Ibid.
167. Bigham, "Icon," pt. 1, para. 1.
168. Ibid., para. 4.
169. Ibid., para. 7.

Any hesitancy regarding the veneration of an icon on the part of Christians today may have more to do with reluctance toward making an outward show of physical gestures rather than misunderstanding the difference between veneration and worship or a deprecation of matter. Christians understand that the same gesture can have different meanings, depending on the circumstances.[170] A bow that honors God and a bow that honors an icon can in fact interiorly be two different gestures. Another basic point that is fairly easily accepted by all Christians is that "any portrait, including one of Christ, does not represent a nature of whatever kind [human or divine], but first and foremost a person in the visible aspects of his humanity."[171] An icon does not presume to represent all that Christ is, both human and divine. As with a likeness of any other person, we do not assume that the likeness can portray everything that a man or woman is, even though it can portray his or her physical likeness, and through that likeness perhaps a small portion of the depths that go beyond their physical appearance.

The third part of Bigham's series points toward a few more problematic areas. One of the arguments of the iconoclasts stated that because the New Testament does not explicitly endorse religious images they should be rejected. However, by supporting icons, Nicaea II demonstrates the understanding that "the Scriptures [are] an expression, though not exhaustive, of the oral Tradition of the Church."[172] Bigham explains that among Christians today, the relationship between Scripture and tradition is an area in which there is a lack of unity. However, he argues, on the whole, Christians today would side with the positions of the iconophiles rather than the iconoclasts. On the question of the validity of icons, "the vast majority of Christians today are orthodox—that is, in agreement with the Scriptures—and can thus proclaim one faith regarding Christian images."[173] Therefore, the challenge actually lies in how the renewed interest in the icon is unfolding among Catholics and Protestants today.

In the latter part of his series, Bigham discusses some of the areas specifically pertaining to Christian art that do divide the Orthodox point of view from that of other Christians. He begins part 4 of the series with extensive quotations from the document on the liturgy from the Second Vatican Council, *Sacrosanctum Concilium*. Using these passages, he points

---

170. Ibid., para. 13.
171. Bigham, "Icon," pt. 2, para. 11.
172. Bigham, "Icon," pt. 3, para. 1.
173. Ibid., para. 6.

out that many Christians, including Catholics, state that the church "has not produced or adopted any particular, specific, artistic style and that it is open to all tastes, to all manners of representing the events and people of salvation history."[174] He points out that while artistic expressions are certainly subject to standards of decency, most Christians would say that as long as those standards are not violated, any style may be, at least theoretically, acceptable.

Bigham explains that he is laying down an opposing viewpoint. The Orthodox Church "claims there is a universal, canonical iconography," even when it is expressed through different historical periods or in different geographical locations.[175] During its first millennia, the church worked out the visual language that expresses the faith that was also worked out in the verbal language of the Scriptures, the councils, and theologians. As is often stated, the icon is theology in line and color, and like theology written in words, it also has the potential to "betray the faith and be designated heretical."[176] The liturgical artist, whether he or she works in iconography or focuses on vestments, furnishings, or other objects, is working for the church and offers an expression of its faith through their skill. The art is not and should not simply be the product of the artist's imagination.

However, throughout Christian history this understanding has not always been respected. Even within the Orthodox Church, icons have sometimes been modeled after Renaissance art rather than the canonical iconographic tradition. "Instead of continuing to paint eschatological images for an eschatological people," explains Bigham, "Orthodox painters adopted the criteria of those who sought to represent this present world and its inhabitants using artistic means . . . which are appropriate for imaging our fallen world."[177] The images of the kingdom were lost, and even as the canonical icon has been rediscovered among Orthodox and non-Orthodox alike, the faithful are not always prepared to use those images in place of the Renaissance images with which they are more accustomed. However, and again in both Orthodox and non-Orthodox churches, canonical iconography continues to be rediscovered, resulting in "artists of every orientation

---

174. Bigham, "Icon," pt. 4, para. 4.
175. Ibid., para. 6.
176. Ibid., para. 7.
177. Bigham, "Icon," pt. 5, para. 2.

who paint, who want to paint, dare to paint icons," using images that may or may not be in keeping with the canonical iconographic tradition.[178]

As actions like this take place, Bigham points out, people ask if or propose that the icon has a place in the restoration of Christian unity. He writes:

> There are even those who say that the icon is God's instrument for uniting the churches. Perhaps this is true, but is this hope well-founded? From this question stems the title of my reflection, "The Icon: Sign of Unity or Division?" The title could also have been "The Ecumenical Importance of the Icon." To what point in fact, can the icon serve as an instrument for Christian unity?[179]

Bigham's statement is similar to the title of this book, and his answer to these questions is key as we move into the section on contributing to the iconographic tradition. That section is part of the journey to Orthodoxy that I described in the introduction, and it also represents well the Orthodox approach to ecumenism that was discussed above. Bigham explains that as more non-Orthodox Christians see, pray with, and learn about the icon, the more they will also experience Orthodox teaching and theology. They will experience the faith that developed when the church was more unified. If their time with canonical iconography leads non-Orthodox Christians to a greater understanding of the faith that, earlier in Christian history, enabled Christians to celebrate a common Eucharist, then this is certainly a reason to support the ecumenical work of the icon.

According to the Russian iconographer Leonid Ouspensky, while the West has not participated in the icon as wholly as the East, the tradition is developing and "now it is the turn of the West to express itself in sacred painting."[180] Rather than iconographers in the West creating work that essentially looks as if it came from Russia, they will eventually need to incorporate their own culture into the iconographic tradition in an appropriate manner. For Ouspensky this would naturally need to include a return to Orthodoxy in the West. When his interviewer states that the spirit of the icon and the spirit of the West are so far apart, Ouspensky responds, "Oh, you know, the spirit . . . it changes, it changes."[181]

---

178. Ibid., para. 3.
179. Ibid.
180. Ouspensky, *Theology in Color*, 25.
181. Ibid.

The icon, Bigham points out, could be taken up as no more than one among many artistic styles or even as being nothing more than a fad. To truly be a part of Christian unity, the icon must move beyond being just one option for personal prayer or home altars; it must regain "its liturgical and dogmatic place in the churches."[182] Bigham concludes that at this point it remains unseen as to whether that will occur, and that while we don't have a complete answer to the question of the ecumenical work of the icon, we can "work, hope, pray, and wait."[183] This book is a part of each of those ways of keeping vigil, of keeping the faith.

---

182. Bigham, "Icon," pt. 6, para. 3.
183. Ibid., para. 4.

2

Contributing to the Conversation
The Iconographic Tradition

An iconographer who takes this work seriously knows that he, or she, is just an apprentice in training. And nothing more.

—Archimandrite Zinon

THROUGH THE FIRST CHAPTER, we have entered the conversation of the ecumenical movement. We have gained an understanding of how the Roman Catholic Church and the Orthodox Church approach ecumenical work. Through consideration of receptive ecumenism, we have gained a stance we may take toward working with Catholic seminarians and other students of the icon. This stance includes a deep respect for the Orthodox Church and a willingness to take responsibility for our own learning about the icon so that learning is not dependent on reciprocity from others, even though such reciprocity is certainly desirable. With that stance in mind, this chapter explores some of the theology, history, and aesthetics of the icon that I have learned thus far and will provide additional groundwork for chapter 3, inviting others into the conversation of the icon. In order to lay some additional groundwork for the invitations that I have offered within the context of a Catholic seminary, I also include some comments in chapter 2 concerning the importance of this material for students who are studying for the priesthood, as well as its importance for students of the Iconographic Arts Institute. More broadly though, the material in this chapter applies to any group with whom I might work through the icon, formally or informally. In this respect, I consider all of us students of the icon.

My aim in this chapter is to be clear. The iconographic tradition is long and rich and deep, and at the time of this writing I am nine years into my study of that tradition. A lifetime of this work would bring a richness that I can only imagine. Therefore, I do not intend this section to speak to each and every area that could be discussed as a part of the iconographic tradition. My goal is to explain as clearly as I can the essential contours of the iconographic tradition that I have learned thus far for the purpose of sharing that tradition with others.

I will outline the basic aesthetics and theology of the icon before discussing some of the history of the icon. I have placed the aesthetics and theology first because part of the history of the icon involves persecution of those who make and venerate icons. With the aesthetics and theology first, we will have a better understanding as to why defending the icon was and is of importance to Christianity.

Before considering specific aspects of the iconographic canon, discussing the nature of tradition as explained by Vladimir Lossky in the book he wrote with Leonid Ouspensky, *The Meaning of Icons*, may be helpful. Lossky was a close friend and colleague of Ouspensky and one of the most well-known Orthodox theologians of the twentieth century. In an essay from *The Meaning of Icons* entitled "Tradition and Traditions," Lossky outlines several points that offer more context for the content of the canon discussed below.

Early in his essay, Lossky differentiates between tradition and the revelation we receive from Scripture. Tradition is the energy and the insight that allows each of us and the church as a whole to understand the revelation we have received. Tradition is "not the word," he explains, "but the living breath which makes the word heard at the same time as the silence from which it came; it is not the Truth, but a communication of the Spirit of Truth."[1] Part of the understanding that tradition brings to the church is the essential connection between tradition and Scripture, one that is "indissoluble and distinct," explains Lossky.[2] Additionally, tradition is not frozen in the external expression or wording of particular practices. "The dynamism of the Tradition," explains Lossky, "allows of no inertia either in

1. Ouspensky and Lossky, *Meaning of Icons*, 16.
2. Ibid.

the habitual forms of piety, or in the dogmatic expressions that are repeated mechanically like magical recipes of Truth."[3] This is an important point for those who are considering the connections between contemporary icons and their prototypes as they begin their study of Orthodox iconography. Working from a prototype is not a matter of copying but of creating a new translation of a particular image, and skilled iconographers can design new icons while still remaining within and respectful of the canon.

Lossky also differentiates among Scripture, tradition, and expressions of tradition, such as dogmas and iconography. These explanations are helpful to students of the icon because Scripture and the icon are often compared to each other. Lossky explains that both dogmas and Scripture "live in the Tradition," but that the Scriptures are a closed canon while the dogmatic tradition may increase by formulating necessary, new expressions of the faith, while still remaining faithful to revealed Truth.[4] He goes on to explain that just as the dogmatic tradition can develop, so can "other expressions of the Christian mystery that the Church produces in the Tradition," including iconography.[5] The iconographic tradition "receives its full meaning and its intimate coherence with other documents of the faith (Scripture, dogmas, liturgy) in the Tradition of the Holy Spirit."[6] Lossky explains that icons may be as intimately connected to Scripture as dogmas since icons proclaim in line and color "what the word announces in written letters."[7] Overall, Lossky's essay clarifies the relationship between the closed canon of the Scriptures and the developing tradition of iconography and the relationship of both to tradition.

The Theology of the Icon

In his book *Techniques of Icon and Wall Painting*, Aidan Hart gives an excellent and concise summary of the theology of the icon on which all of the technical elements are based. First and foremost, the theological basis for the icon is the Incarnation of Jesus Christ.[8] God became a man in Jesus of Nazareth, a man that people could see, hear, smell, and touch; therefore,

3. Ibid., 19.
4. Ibid., 21.
5. Ibid., 22.
6. Ibid.
7. Ibid.
8. Hart, *Techniques*, 2.

we can portray his humanity in an icon, just as we could any other person. Hart's second point is intimately linked to the Incarnation. The material world is good and at the same time should not be unnecessarily privileged over the spiritual world. God reaches humanity and saves us through the material world, through our senses.[9] As we are healed we are deified, transfigured; we become God by grace.[10]

The rest of Hart's points build on the Incarnation and the goodness of the material world. First, he describes the writing of an icon as "priestly work" because the iconographer uses the materials of nature and lifts them to a "higher plane."[11] As will be discussed below, the iconographer can do this while maintaining the distinction between the veneration given to an image of Christ and his saints and the worship due to God alone.[12] Hart also speaks of the icon as initiator; through the priestly work of the iconographer the viewer is brought into a spiritual reality that often seems hidden. This experience corresponds to the experience of the apostles during the Transfiguration of Christ. Through the glory of Christ's presence, Peter, James, and John saw and felt the true spiritual meaning of Christ and the world.[13] In addition to the reality of Christ, viewers may also experience the reality of the communion of saints. Through the icon, we are in the presence of fellow members of the body of Christ, those who went before us and pray for us now through our struggles and our joys.[14]

Communion in Christ is also central to Hart's next point. Iconography is fundamentally a liturgical art, and liturgical art is by its very nature at the service of the community's worship and prayer. The presence of an icon in a church or chapel, a room of one's home, or a public place indicates that place is a place of prayer.[15] It brings together the earthy reality of an individual and community's daily activities and the spiritual reality of Christ. Lastly, Hart speaks of the mission of the icon. As a liturgical art, the icon is primarily intended for members of the church. However, the icon may also be a means of conversion for those who are more peripherally connected

---

9. Ibid., 4.
10. Ibid., 3.
11. Ibid., 4.
12. Ibid.
13. Ibid., 5.
14. Ibid., 4.
15. Ibid., 3.

to the church as well.[16] When we have the mission of the icon, we have the ministry of beauty.

Hart explains that all of these elements of the theology of the icon are used in all of the schools of iconography that have developed throughout Christian history, whether they be in Greece, Russia, or in the West. These schools have built the aesthetics of the icon on the theology of the icon. Each school, "when it is spiritually healthy, operates according to the timeless principles but also seeks to affirm these by absorbing the appropriate elements of the surrounding culture."[17] This echoes Ouspensky's point about iconographers in the West, who eventually need to be creating icons that are more than copies of Russian icons. When iconographers use the timeless principles Hart describes, they are respecting the iconographic canon. Hart explains that every icon should contain a transfigured world, not a naturalistic world, a world that the viewer understands through their spiritual as well as the physical senses. The structure of the figures and other elements in an icon respect natural anatomy and then abstract from it so as to emphasize the spiritual nature of the subject. The perspective system should shape the experience of viewing so that the more important figures come out toward the viewer.[18] Secondary figures and elements should be in service of the primary elements such as the major figures and faces of Christ, the Mother of God, and the saints. Gold assist, the lines of gold leaf used on garments and other objects, should be used "to indicate transfigured matter and not as mere ornament."[19] With each of these principles in place, the mission and the beauty of the icon can move forward.

In his book *Orthodox Iconography*, Constantine Cavarnos also discusses several functions of the icon in the life of the church, functions that can add more detail to our understanding of the mission of the icon. He explains that icons increase the beauty of the church in which the faithful worship, a point he illustrates with a hymn for the evening before the Sunday of Orthodoxy: "The Church of Christ is now embellished like a bride, having been adorned with icons of holy form; and it calls all together spiritually; let us come and celebrate together joyfully with concord and faith, magnifying the Lord."[20] Cavarnos reminds his readers that all of the beauty of the church

---

16. Ibid., 5.
17. Ibid., *Techniques*, xx.
18. Ibid., 30.
19. Ibid.
20. Cavarnos, *Orthodox Iconography*, 30.

and the liturgy is at the service of the spiritual reality of Christ and of the Holy Trinity. It is never simply for the sake of beauty itself.

Cavarnos also discusses the instruction of the faithful. Icons teach just as the Scriptures do. When more of the general population was illiterate, icons provided instruction for those who could not read, and according to Cavarnos, an icon can be an even more vivid means of instruction than the written word. Even when the faithful have received instruction, they can forget what they have learned and "become preoccupied with everyday worldly matters and pursuits."[21] As we pray with an icon, we may remember the commandments, the Beatitudes, and the spiritual reality of the world. As we remember, we can be lifted "to the prototypes, to a higher level of consciousness, of thought and feeling."[22] Images of Christ and his saints bring us back to our faith and move us to strive for their virtues. As we do so, we are sanctified.

Ouspensky explains in *The Meaning of Icons* that iconography, as is true of all theology, tries to express the divine reality through a human instrument, and ultimately that expression is going to fail. "There are no words, nor colours nor lines, which could represent the Kingdom of God," he explains, "as we represent and describe our world."[23] Both theology and iconography ultimately fail at their task, but Ouspensky argues that failure is also the strength of theology and iconography because they both push to the limits of human knowledge and ability. The language of the icon becomes figurative and symbolic, just as the Scriptures take on the language of the parables.[24] An icon can bring the viewer closer to God, yet there will always be more, a fuller experience and understanding of God that is yet come.

The Vocation of the Iconographer

The primary audience for this book, the students and faculty of Catholic seminaries, understand and have experienced a sense of calling. They understand that a calling to a particular state of life or kind of work comes from God and builds on the talents they have and the circumstances in which they live. Depending on their experience with the icon or the arts

21. Ibid., 32.
22. Ibid.
23. Ouspensky and Lossky, *Meaning of Icons*, 48.
24. Ibid., 49.

before I work with them, they may not understand that an iconographer seriously discerns his or her calling as well.

As a vocation, the work of iconography is a spiritual work, a service offered from within and to the church. Irina Yazykova explains that the "church fathers considered the true writing of icons, 'the art of arts,' to be the process of doing spiritual work. It is this work that cleans and blesses and transfigures us."[25] During the opening gathering of the institute each year, the instructors of the institute emphasize this point. Of course each of you is writing an icon on a board this week, they explain, yet at the same time there is an icon being written in each of you, and we are writing an icon of community as the students, instructors, staff, and wider community move through the week together.

Leonid Ouspensky and one of his students, Father Patrick Doolan, an Orthodox priest and monk now residing in California, have both discussed elements of the iconographer's vocation. First, Ouspensky offers some of the contours of the vocation of the iconographer. Ouspensky, like Yazykova, explains that the vocation of the iconographer is a call to a participation in prayer and the very life of the church. This point may be particularly important for students who are discerning a vocation as a Catholic priest. These men need to understand that an iconographer experiences a discernment process and needs to sustain a life of prayer just as they do. Without that discernment and commitment to prayer, Ouspensky explains, the image ceases to be an icon. "No artistic fantasy, no perfection of technique, no artistic gift can replace actual knowledge," he explains.[26] This does not mean, of course, that a person has to be perfect and totally sanctified in order to write an icon. According to Ouspensky, "every Orthodox iconographer, living in the Tradition, can make genuine icons."[27] Here Ouspensky means Orthodox in the strict sense of a member of the Orthodox Church, a point with which those of us who discern a call to iconography and who are not Orthodox must struggle. This is part of the work we do through receptive ecumenism. However, Ouspensky's point still has validity for non-Orthodox iconographers. Prayer and the life of faith make an image an icon.

The prayer and faith of the iconographer is built on his or her life within the church and the taking up of tradition as previously discussed by

25. Yazykova, *Hidden and Triumphant*, 11.
26. Ouspensky and Lossky, *Meaning of Icons*, 42.
27. Ibid.

Lossky. Tradition brings each new generation the "actual fact of existence of an icon," and it also gives an "inexhaustible fountain of knowledge communicated to the Church by the Holy Spirit."[28] The communication from the Holy Spirit, the revelation of Jesus Christ, is the content of the work of the iconographer. He must be immersed in the life of the church so as to be a faithful witness to Jesus Christ. Ouspensky explains:

> In order to receive and pass on the testimony, the iconographer must not only believe that it is genuine, but must also share in the life, by which the witness of the revelation lives, must follow the same way, that is, be a member of the body of the Church. Only then can he transmit the testimony received consciously and exactly.[29]

The iconographer works from within the tradition and works to allow the tradition to penetrate every part of her life and work. While the iconographer must make many decisions regarding aesthetics and practical matters as she works on an icon, she does so from within the iconographic canon. The images made through the hand of an iconographer are not her personal creation or vision; they are a witness to the revelation we have received through Jesus Christ.

The iconographer is also held to a high moral standard and a life of asceticism, a life Ouspensky characterizes as monastic: "For a true iconographer, creation is the way of asceticism and prayer, that is an essentially monastic way."[30] Through her asceticism, the iconographer is overcoming her own desires, her own subjective way of approaching the work of writing an icon, as well as her reasons for writing it. She does not write it to express her own creativity or artistic point of view; rather she works at the behest of and in service to the church and for the glory of God. The practice of not signing an icon as other pieces of artwork are signed is an external expression of this understanding of service and asceticism.[31] The iconographer finds her true spiritual freedom by working within the tradition. Technical skill has an important place, but it does not always determine the ultimate quality of the work. "An icon may be technically perfect but of a very low spiritual level," explains Ouspensky, "and conversely, there are icons roughly and primitively painted which stand on a very high spiritual

---

28. Ibid.
29. Ibid.
30. Ibid.
31. Ibid.

level."[32] We should particularly keep this point in mind as we move through the more technical aspects of iconography below.

When Ouspensky first started working with his student Patrick Doolan, Ouspensky said to him, "You're going to stop this tracing and you're going to start to learn to draw on your own and learn the artistic language of the icon."[33] Doolan explains that Ouspensky understood that Doolan's primary teachers are the ancient icons themselves, the theology and technique of which is passed from the master to his or her apprentice. Doolan speaks beautifully of the relationship between the apprentice and the master iconographer. He explains that once he started working with Ouspensky, he knew it could last a lifetime or for as long as Ouspensky was willing to work with him. When it comes to training in iconography, a solid master and apprentice relationship provides the best setting for learning the tradition. Ouspensky passed on to Doolan "his sense of being part of the Church and icon painting as being an expression of the Church."[34] Now Doolan works with his own students "with the understanding that what we're doing is testing a vocation."[35] That testing isn't necessarily about the person's talent but about their seriousness about the work. In the Orthodox tradition, an iconographer's vocation is affirmed through the blessing of a bishop. After he had studied with Ouspensky for several years, Ouspensky took him to the bishop for his blessing, for the blessing and recognition by the church of his work.

Doolan also describes the humility and repentance that develops as an iconographer's commitment to his work deepens. "It's a rather terrifying thing to think that one's icons are going to go into the prayer life of individuals," he explains, and "you have to be quite fearful of the whole enterprise and most iconographers are, I think."[36] Doolan brings that healthy fear back to the necessity of prayer and the need for iconographers in the church today. An iconographer's work is difficult, and there is a high demand for icons; therefore, the relationship of prayer between the iconographer and the community for whom an icon is intended is essential. Through the prayer of the church, the iconographer is able to offer new icons to the faithful.

32. Ibid., 43.
33. Doolan, "CIVA Interviews," 1.
34. Ibid., 2.
35. Ibid., 3.
36. Ibid., 6.

The Icon and the Liturgy

As explained above by Aidan Hart, iconography is a liturgical art that serves the worship and prayer of the Christian community. Every portion of the liturgical arts, architecture, music, vestments, furnishings, and iconography are woven together; thus the icon is inseparable from the other liturgical arts and from the liturgy as a whole. As the icon has been reintroduced in the West, the primary experience of the icon for many Christians has been the use of an icon in their personal prayer and devotions. Some may have experienced icons within their churches, while others may have also seen icons placed in areas of the church or parish buildings that are less conducive to silence and prayer. The primary home of the icon is the church itself; other placements and uses flow from the icon as experienced in the liturgy.

While consideration of each of the liturgical arts falls outside the scope of this book, a comment from Leonid Ouspensky illustrates how one element cannot be separated from the others. Before he was a believer, he stepped inside an Orthodox church and gazed at an icon while also hearing the choir chanting: "So I listened to that singing, I looked at that icon, I was completely stunned. I could see absolutely the same structure, the same movements, the same lines; I was terribly shaken. It frightened me."[37] We must keep in mind the fundamental unity of the liturgical arts, even though iconography is our primary focus.

The Church Building

In addition to the iconostasis, which will be discussed below, there is a particular scheme for the layout of the icons in an Orthodox church. When other Christian churches and communities consider icons for their churches, they should keep this layout in mind, but not necessarily for the purpose of directly imitating it. An understanding of this layout will help those responsible to make informed decisions about iconography that respects the Orthodox iconographic tradition while also taking their own community's circumstances into account.

In his book *Orthodox Iconography*, Constantine Cavarnos gives a clear explanation of the arrangement of the icons in an Orthodox church. Orthodox churches are usually domed churches, as compared to the churches in the West that are modeled on the basilica. The layout he describes is suitable

---

37. Ouspensky, *Theology in Color*, 21.

for a large domed church; iconographers who are working with spaces that are not domed or are much smaller would make the necessary adjustments. The topmost portion of the dome is dedicated to the Pantocrator, Christ the Ruler of All, the largest image in the church. The Pantocrator is a large bust of Christ holding the Gospel book in his left hand and blessing with his right hand. When the dome is large enough, the Mother of God and St. John the Forerunner appear below the iris of the dome. Between the windows of the dome are the Old Testament prophets, and below the prophets on the four triangles between the arches supporting the dome are the four evangelists.[38] After the dome, the most important part of the iconography in the church is the eastern apse.

In the semi-dome of the apse is the Mother of God with the Christ child in front of her or on her lap, depending on the size of the figure. Sometimes the Archangels Michael and Gabriel will be on either side of her.[39] Below the Mother of God is an image of the Divine Liturgy. This image includes a vested Christ who is assisted by angels who are also vested. Below the image of the Divine Liturgy is an image of Christ giving communion to his disciples. As space permits, the lowest part of the apse contains images of the hierarchs who are also dressed for the Divine Liturgy, including St. Basil, St. Gregory Nazianzen, St. John Chrysostom, and St. Athanasius the Great.[40] The narthex of the church often includes an image of Christ the Teacher over the main entrance, with the Theotokos and St. John the Forerunner on either side of him. The rest of the narthex includes a variety of images, including those from the life of the Mother of God, the lives of the martyrs, visions from Revelation, and other busts and standing figures of individual saints.[41]

The above describes the inside of the church, but of course the outside of the domes are beautiful and striking as well. The onion domes of Russia seem to be a structure that draws from the spiritual world we are immersed in through the Divine Liturgy. In his book *Icons: Theology in Color*, Eugene N. Trubetskoi describes the Russian domes as a candle flame topped by a cross:

> Looking at the Ivan Velikii belfry in Moscow, we see, as it were, a gigantic candle burning in the Moscow skies. The many-domed

38. Cavarnos, *Orthodox Iconography*, 24–26.
39. Ibid., 27.
40. Ibid., 28.
41. Ibid.

Kremlin cathedrals and churches are like enormous candle holders full of candles. And it is not the golden domes alone that express this idea of surging prayer. When you look from afar, in bright sunlight, at an old Russian monastery or a city with many churches, all of it seems to glow with multicolored lights. And when these lights sparkle distantly in a great field of snow, they draw you like a faraway, otherworldly vision of the City of God.[42]

The whole church, exterior and interior, brings the kingdom of God to us and teaches us how to live in that kingdom with all the saints.

The Iconostasis

Aidan Hart provides a clear explanation of the iconostasis to accompany Cavarnos's description of the church building as a whole. He explains that as Christian worship developed, there always was some kind of marker between the sanctuary where the Eucharist takes place and the nave where the congregation gathers. By the time of the fall of Constantinople, a larger wooden screen stood between the sanctuary and the narthex; the screen extended the width of the church from north to south and had several levels or tiers. As the iconostasis developed in Russia, it could extend up to five tiers.[43] According to Ouspensky, while we read the iconostasis as the boundary between the world of divinity and the world of humanity, the iconostasis also brings humanity and divinity together through the images that reveal how the reconciliation of the two is achieved.[44]

At a minimum, an iconostasis consists of two stands, one with an icon of Christ and one with an icon of the Mother of God. A large iconostasis can have up to five tiers and contain as many as fifty different icons.[45] One of the best explanations and illustrations of the scheme for the iconostasis that I have found is from *The Meaning of Icons*, by Leonid Ouspensky and Vladimir Lossky. More detailed theological discussion is found in Ouspensky's two-volume work, *The Theology of the Icon*. The material from *The Meaning of Icons* includes a simple line drawing that illustrates the placement of the icons within the iconostasis. Ouspensky's explanation is accompanied by photographs of a fifteenth-century iconostasis in the side chapel of the

---

42. Trubetskoi, *Icons*, 17.
43. Hart, *Techniques*, 67.
44. Ouspensky and Lossky, *Meaning of Icons*, 60.
45. Hart, *Techniques*, 67.

Nativity of the Theotokos in the St. Sophia Cathedral of Novgorod and a smaller portable iconostasis, also Russian and from the fifteenth century. Ouspensky explains that the portable iconostasis contains the three rows of the "tchin" or *deisis*, the icons of the liturgical feasts, and the row of the prophets, which is the traditional arrangement for an iconostasis. A church iconostasis includes a lower section with local icons, the Royal Door, the north door, and the south door, and an additional top tier of the Old Testament forefathers. For the rest of this section on the iconostasis, I draw upon Ouspensky's material and will outline his points concerning each row or section mentioned above.

Icons of the Prophets

This upper row of a three-tiered iconostasis contains icons of Old Testament prophets, each with an open scroll in his hand. The scroll contains words from their writing that pertain to the Incarnation. In the middle of the row of prophets is the icon of the Mother of God of the Sign, "the image of the Divine Incarnation as the fulfillment of their prophecies."[46] The posture and gestures of the prophets vary, indicating that each prophesied about the Incarnation in his own way. The Mother of God of the Sign in the center of the row is a bridge among the prophets on either side of her, the Old Testament forefathers above her in a larger iconostasis, and the figures representing the New Testament below her.[47] From the point of view of standing in front of the iconostasis, the order of the prophets in Ouspensky's example is David, Zacharias, Moses, Samuel, Nahum, Daniel, and Habakkuk to the left of the Mother of God of the Sign, and Solomon, Ezekiel, Haggai, Elias, Malachi, Elisha, and Zechariah to her right.

Icons of the Liturgical Feasts

The row below the prophets represents the major feasts of the liturgical year that are based on the events in the New Testament, feasts that "are celebrated by the Church with particular solemnity, as the principal stages of the action of the Divine Providence in the world," and the fulfillment of the images portrayed in the rows of the Old Testament prophets and

---

46. Ouspensky and Lossky, *Meaning of Icons*, 63.
47. Ibid.

forefathers.⁴⁸ This row usually contains the icon of the Resurrection and twelve other feasts. The six feasts of the Lord are the Nativity, Candlemas (Presentation), Epiphany (Baptism), the Transfiguration, the Entry into Jerusalem, and the Ascension. The four feasts of the Mother of God are her Nativity, her Presentation, the Annunciation, and the Assumption. The last two feasts are Pentecost and the Elevation of the Cross. These feasts are usually arranged in the order that they occur during the liturgical year according to the Orthodox calendar. Space permitting, icons of other liturgical feasts and of the Crucifixion may also be included in this row.

The Tchin (or *Deisis*)

The row below the liturgical feasts is the *deisis*; *deisis* is the Greek for prayer, and "in this case, the standing in prayer, before the Saviour, of the Mother of God, and of John the Baptist."⁴⁹ Because the figures in this row represent the resurrected Christ and his saints, it is the most important part of the iconostasis and is the fulfillment of the rows above it. Christ Enthroned is in the middle of the row with the Mother of God on his right and John the Baptist on his left. *Tchin* means "order" and refers to the order of the icons in this row that represent different categories of saints, such as angels, apostles, and hierarchs. In Ouspensky's example, after the Mother of God are Michael the Archangel, the Apostle Peter, Saint Basil the Great, Saint John Chrysostom, Saint Zossima, and the martyr George. After John the Baptist are Gabriel the Archangel, the Apostle Paul, Saint Gregory the Theologian, Saint Nicholas, Saint Sabbatius, and the martyr Demetrius. In contrast to the busts of the prophets and forefathers above them, these saints have a common posture and gesture as their full standing figures turn toward Christ in the middle of the row.⁵⁰ Their common postures represent the good order of the universe directed toward Christ. Ouspensky explains that this order is also "the image of attainment of the normal order of the universe, the order of the life to come, where 'God' is 'all in all' (I Cor. xv. 28), the contemplation of Divine Glory."⁵¹ In the image of Christ

48. Ibid.
49. Ibid.
50. Ibid., 64.
51. Ibid.

Enthroned, Christ is "surrounded by heavenly powers" and gold rays of light emanate from him.[52]

The Worship Storey and the Royal Door

This row, which is below the *deisis* and at the eye level of the viewer, differs from church to church and does not necessarily have the same "rhythmic arrangement" as the other rows.[53] In the middle of the row is the Royal Door. To the left of the viewer is a large icon of the Savior, and to the right of the viewer is a large icon of the Virgin and Child. The icon of the Savior may be replaced with an icon of the feast or the patron saint of the church. The Archangels Michael and Gabriel or deacons who are saints appear behind the Savior and the Virgin and Child as servers for the Divine Liturgy.[54]

The Royal Door is composed of a hinged double door containing icons of the Evangelists and several other images. As the door that leads to the sanctuary, the Royal Door stands for the entrance into the kingdom of God, and it is used only by the clergy and only at certain times during the Divine Liturgy. The icons on the Royal Door portray those who announced the kingdom, and they appear in the following arrangement: with the viewer standing in front of the Royal Door the Annunciation appears in two parts, one on each leaf of the door. The Archangel Gabriel is on the left and the Mother of God is on the right. Below the Archangel Gabriel are Saint John and Saint Luke, and below the Mother of God are Saint Matthew and Saint Mark.

An image of Christ giving communion to the apostles at the Last Supper appears above the Royal Door. This image is a liturgical interpretation of the historical moment that Christ established the Eucharist. The image is a double portrayal of Christ distributing communion, once with the bread and once with the cup.[55] It appears directly above the place outside of the Royal Door where the faithful will receive communion from today's successors of the apostles.[56]

---

52. Ibid.
53. Ibid.
54. Ibid., 66.
55. Ibid., 67.
56. Ibid.

The Iconographic Canon

This section includes some of the basic material that Catholic seminarians and all students of the icon need to understand about the aesthetic elements of an icon. Much of this material is drawn from *The Icon: Image of the Invisible*, by Father Egon Sendler, SJ, one of the teachers of Mary Katsilometes and Kathy Sievers, two of the primary instructors for the Iconographic Arts Institute. He draws his teaching from the study of the ancient icons that serve as the prototypes for icons that are painted today. We will consider these in the general order that an iconographer needs to work with them as she works on an icon.

At first glance, and particularly for those who are more accustomed to working with contemporary art, the iconographic canon may seem restrictive. However, as Irina Yazykova explains, the canon should not be viewed as "an iron cage" but rather as the "central core of meanings that ensure that the icon image is filled with the appropriate doctrinal and theological content."[57] She compares the iconographic canon to a tree: "It is rooted, along with Orthodox tradition, in the soil of Holy Scripture. We might consider its trunk the Orthodox Holy Tradition, and its branches the nations and localities that gave rise to the various schools and master iconographers."[58] The aesthetic elements of iconography take up the everyday appearance and organization of the world and then alter it to depict the kingdom of God: "We submit this form to a special geometric, rhythmic, and chromatic system which is more capable of suggesting interiority, that is the spiritual and divine essence."[59] That system, the details of which we will explore below, helps to put our human experience in touch with the divine.

Geometry

Sacred geometry provides the scaffolding that supports the drawing and painting of an icon. The proportions in an icon are usually simple, with the proportions 3:4 and 4:5 predominating because of the knowledge ancient iconographers had of the sacred triangle.[60] Thirty percent of ancient icons were 3:4, 30 percent were 4:5, and 10 percent had other proportions such

---

57. Yazykova, *Hidden and Triumphant*, 5.
58. Ibid., 10.
59. Sendler, *Icon*, 117–18.
60. Ibid., 87.

as 2:3, 5:7, and 5:6. For standing figures, which will be discussed below, the proportions were usually 2:5 or 1:3.[61] Before she begins the drawing that serves as the basis for painting, the iconographer must do an analysis of the geometry of the prototype for her icon. If she neglects the geometry, those who see that work will be able to sense its ineffectiveness even if they lack an understanding of geometry because the geometry is a major part of what gives an icon a sense of stillness and quiet. At the same time, the placement of the figures and other elements laid over the geometry can be altered to some degree because "the structure suppress[es] neither the movement nor the expression" in the icon.[62] The iconographer guards the core meaning of the icon and makes the appropriate changes.

Sendler explains that different iconographic figures are based on different shapes. Bust figures are based on triangles, standing figures on squares and circles, and festal icons on crosses, grids, and circles. For bust figures, the isosceles triangle "is in perfect symmetry and rests firmly on its base."[63] The shoulders and arms of the figure fill the lower portion of the triangle, with the nose usually in close alignment with the tip at the top of the triangle. Most of the ancient icons of standing figures are located on an iconostasis in rows with other standing figures from a similar category such as apostles, kings, or angels. These figures need a composition that is simple and straightforward in order to be in harmony with one another.[64] In a standing figure with a proportion of 1:3, the bottom third includes the figure roughly from the knees down, and the top third includes most of a figure that would be included in a bust. Generally speaking, the halo and the head create two concentric circles, and the relationship between the two may vary.[65]

The geometry of the festal icons that depict the major feasts of the liturgical year is more complex than that of busts and standing figures. Festal icons were usually not based strictly on a square since this shape is usually not in accord with the human figure.[66] Rather, the geometry for festal icons is based on the cross, the grid, and the circle. As with the simpler figures, the central points of the geometry correspond to the central figures in the icon.

61. Ibid.
62. Ibid., 106.
63. Ibid., 89.
64. Ibid., 94.
65. Ibid., 90.
66. Ibid., 99.

For instance, an icon of the Ascension is based on a cross with Christ above the horizontal line, the Mother of God below the horizontal line and on the vertical line, and the apostles and angels also below the horizontal line and on either side of the Mother of God.[67] The Nativity is an icon based on a grid; the main vertical in the middle of the icon and one of the horizontal lines are central to the organization of the icon, but key figures in the image appear in each square of the grid. The Nativity also demonstrates well how the geometry points the viewer toward the most important parts of the story told by a festal icon. "The real center of the icon [of the Nativity] is the Christ-Child's head which is on the axis of vertical symmetry and connects the star, the Child, and Mary's womb," explains Sendler.[68] The circle is often placed within a square in a festal icon. The circle can be found in icons of the Mystical Supper, the Transfiguration and the Baptism of Christ. Perhaps the most well-known example of the circle is Andre Rublev's icon of the Trinity in which the circle draws the viewer into the unity among the three persons of the Trinity depicted by the three angels.[69]

The iconographer situates the human figures with their own proportions within the larger structures of the triangle, the cross, the grid, and the circle. The human figures are based on an understanding of the module, particularly of the nose and the head.[70] In Byzantine art, the focus on the module rather than on the relations among different parts of the body has given the icon both stability and flexibility. As a "clear canon of measure" the module "produced a stable tradition" and enabled Byzantine art "to keep its distinctive character through many centuries."[71] The nose module is measured from the root of the nose, the portion between the eyes, to the tip of the nose. The nose module serves as the radius of the head module, and then the head module serves to build the figure. Generally speaking, the number of head modules that make up the body has shifted through the centuries. The body was sometimes lengthened, particularly after the fourteenth century.[72] The geometry of the face is based on the nose module and is constructed differently depending on whether the face is frontal or at a three-quarter turn. For a frontal face, the center of the two circles that

---

67. Ibid.
68. Ibid., 101.
69. Ibid., 105.
70. Ibid., 108.
71. Ibid., 109.
72. Ibid., 112.

create the head and the halo indicates the root of the nose. This placement is significant because "the root of the nose is also the center of the head and the seat of wisdom."[73] The pupils of the eyes and the tip of the nose make an equilateral triangle, thus making the face balanced and harmonious.

Perspective is the last part of our consideration of the spatial relationships in an icon. When any artist working on a flat surface takes the reality of three dimensions and creates a work in two dimensions, he or she is creating a system of perspective. The perspective used in iconography is inverse perspective, the perspective in which the vanishing point is not within or behind the image but in front of the image.[74] Inverse perspective is the opposite of linear perspective. In linear perspective, the vanishing point moves away from the viewer to a point behind the surface. Sendler explains that "in the icon . . . space itself becomes active instead of the observer who in fact is acted on."[75] This spiritual world comes out to meet us, to bring us into the beauty and truth of the power and life of God.

Color

After analyzing an icon's spatial relationships through geometry, proportion, and perspective, the iconographer turns to color. The canon guides him in the colors used for each aspect of an image. "The brightness, purity, and nobility of an icon's colors," explains Irina Yazykova, "serve to reflect the incorruptible beauty of eternity itself."[76] Each color is part of bringing that beauty toward the viewer and into the world around her.

Sometimes the use of color follows the natural coloring of objects, such as green for vegetation and brown for earth. For other objects that vary in their coloring, such as garments, the colors used depict more of the theological meaning in an icon. With a proper understanding of color, the iconographer will make sound choices in her work that respect the symbolic value given by the canon and that are also in harmony with color theory. Seminarians and all students of the icon will have a better understanding of the theological content of an icon if they understand the canon's use of color.

---

73. Ibid., 113.
74. Ibid., 127.
75. Ibid.
76. Yazykova, *Hidden and Triumphant*, 9.

Sendler discusses individual colors "according to their capacity to express the properties of the divine essence."[77] Throughout his discussion, Sendler includes the role each color had in the pagan world prior to Christianity and the role each color has in the Scriptures; some of this material will be included in this discussion. Sendler explains that discussing color in iconography can be challenging because of the lack of precise meaning for many terms and because discussions of color are not very prominent in the source materials for iconography. However, he adds, we can still draw some valuable conclusions about the role of various colors and their relationships with one another.[78]

White is associated with purity since it is by definition the absence of all other colors. In the ancient world, white was the color of the gods and those consecrated to them, but the ancient world needed "to receive the Christian revelation, with its visions of light, in order for the color white to acquire a new richness."[79] Optically, white is the color closest to light and is very dynamic; it dominates in an image and is the first area to catch the attention of the viewer. In iconography, white is the color of those "penetrated by the light of God."[80] For instance, Christ in the Transfiguration and the angels in the icon of the Women at the Tomb are dressed in white. Black, the complete opposite of white, is rarely found in icons, though when it is present its strength depicts separation and death. Sendler explains that white represents the purest form of dynamism while "black is the absence of everything, nothing."[81] Black is found in the damned of the Last Judgment, Lazarus's tomb, and the cavern beneath the cross in the Crucifixion.

Blue is next to white in terms of its association with purity and its sense of calm. According to Sendler, it moves beyond all that is earthly, is deep and tranquil, and is "the least sensual and the most spiritual of all the colors."[82] In the Old Testament, the Tent of the Covenant is blue, which illustrates the close connection blue has with the presence of God. Shades of blue most often appear in garments and mandorlas. The garments include the *himation* or cloak wore by the Pantocrator and other images of Christ, some of the clothing of the Mother of God, and the garments of some of

---

77. Sendler, *Icon*, 153.
78. Ibid., 161.
79. Ibid., 153.
80. Ibid., 155.
81. Ibid., 160.
82. Ibid., 155.

the apostles. The mandorlas in icons such as the Transfiguration and the Protecting Veil of the Mother of God are various shades of blue with the darkest shades in the middle; the mandorlas depict the presence of God breaking into the world. This dark blue represents the divine light that is so overpowering it is experienced as darkness.[83]

In contrast to blue, red is a hot, active color that moves toward the viewer. Red is used frequently in iconography, even as the background instead of gold or white because it so easily stands out against other colors. In the Hellenistic world, red did not seem to have much symbolism. "It was in Christianity," explains Sendler, "that red received its consecration by the blood of Christ."[84] In the Old Testament, red is associated with life since blood was so closely associated with life; for instance, the good wife in Proverbs is clothed in red. In the New Testament, the cloak Jesus wears at the Passion is red, showing that he is shedding his blood for the world. Red is also associated with the blood shed by the martyrs and the red of fire such as the red seraphim and the fire in the Last Judgment.[85]

Purple is associated with wealth and power because the dye required to produce it was very expensive in the ancient world. Purple also stands for power since it is associated with consecration; in both Greek literature and the Scriptures dignitaries and kings are dressed in purple. In the Byzantine Empire, emperors were often born in a purple hall of the imperial palace. In iconography, purple is not associated quite as heavily with the threat that often comes with wealth and power, and it usually appears closer to red than distinctly purple. Sendler points out that sometimes the cloak of the Mother of God is described as purple, but it is actually a dark red. He asks, "Might not the ancient purple have lost all its menacing character so as to recall only the richness and the deep peace of God's dignity?"[86] Perhaps this is another instance of the symbolic meaning of a color shifting due to the influence of Christianity.

Green, another calm color after blue, is of course prominent in nature as the color of vegetation. It has come to symbolize hope and fertility in both the Scriptures and secular language. In terms of color theory, green is the complementary color of red. Its calm balances against red's strength and power. In iconography, green is often found against the red of the clothing

---

83. Yazykova, *Hidden and Triumphant*, 9.
84. Sendler, *Icon*, 157.
85. Ibid., 156.
86. Ibid., 158.

of the martyrs, as well as in the clothing of secondary figures in festal icons. This was probably done for artistic as much as symbolic reasons.[87] Brown is also a calm color, even dull in comparison to the others. Overall, brown does not have a symbolic meaning separate from its place as the natural color of the earth, rocks, and buildings.[88]

Light

Gold is the color associated with light in iconography, and it needs to be differentiated from yellow. Pure yellow appears very little in iconography, and when it does, it is associated with events of grief and sadness, such as Christ being placed in the tomb. In contrast to yellow or any other color, gold "is the pure reflection of light, of brilliance."[89] Often when seeing an individual icon for the first time or upon seeing a large group of icons for the first time, such as in the iconostasis of an Orthodox church, one of the first characteristics that strikes the viewer is the gold, the light. This is fitting because icons bring us into the kingdom of God where the light is not the natural light of the sun that shifts and leaves shadows but the spiritual light of the presence of God.

Rather than the people and objects in an icon being illuminated by an outside source, their light comes from within the image. Thus, the light of sanctity is the illumination of the icon. Essentially, gold is placed "everywhere that the participation in the life of God is emphasized."[90] Gold is found in the background of many icons, in halos, in the details of the garments of the saints, as well as in key pieces of furniture, architecture, or other important objects that come in contact with Christ, the Mother of God, or the saints in an icon. Gold filigree, referred to as gold assist, is used to create lines on garments and other objects. Thin white lines used to highlight the face, hands, and other areas of the flesh, referred to as *dvizhki* lines, are also used.[91]

Irina Yazykova explains that because light is the primary element indicating the transcendent and because honoring that principle includes the exclusion of shadow in an icon, the slow diminishment of light and the

87. Ibid., 159.
88. Ibid., 160.
89. Ibid., 161.
90. Ibid., 172.
91. Yazykova, *Hidden and Triumphant*, 8.

growth of the shadows is an indication that the icon has become degraded, that it no longer adheres to the iconographic canon. She explains that in Russian iconography of the seventeenth and eighteenth centuries, this light of transcendence, of God, "came to be replaced by naturalistic use of light and shade."[92] When this occurs, the image is no longer truly an icon.

Eugene Trubetskoi also gives a lovely and poetic explanation of the use of color in Russian iconography by describing the place each one has in a beautiful sky. Through his description, we may consider color in iconography as solar "in that word's highest spiritual sense."[93] The bright sun at midday crowns the top of the solar hierarchy; every other color has a place in iconography, but "only the solar gold symbolizes the *center* of divine life. All the rest are its environment."[94] The bright ray of the sun, of divine life, is refracted through the rest of nature, through all the rest of the colors of the rainbow. The lines of gold assist become a beautiful web of "fine rays emitted by God and lighting everything around."[95] The world of nature, the sun and everything it touches, is transfigured into the kingdom of God.

The Line in Iconography

Two main components of any composition, including an icon, are color and line. To learn about line in iconography, we can turn to George Kordis and his book *Icon as Communion*. As the iconographer starts his work, he may encounter line first as he begins working on his drawing after analyzing the geometry. However, he also may have worked on color when he selected his prototype. According to Kordis, color precedes line because line gives form to color; line in iconography is "inconceivable independent of color."[96] Line gives the areas of color their definition and moves the color toward the viewer. Kordis explains that it is "line that gives hypostasis [essence] to Byzantine art, i.e., that distinguishes it from any other tradition."[97] Essentially, the role of the line is to give more specificity to color, to give shape to the various colors, and thus to serve "both their intercommunion

---

92. Ibid.
93. Trubetskoi, *Icons*, 48.
94. Ibid.
95. Ibid., 49.
96. Kordis, *Icon as Communion*, 5.
97. Ibid., 6.

and the relationship of the work to the beholder."[98] In this way, line is the element that draws together all of the other elements of the icon, including the viewer himself, through the action and energy it enables the forms to exert toward other forms and the viewer.

The line keeps the various forms from conflicting with one another; it simplifies and purifies the forms.[99] Line creates the movement of the transverse principle, the principle that the lines should move horizontally across the surface in such a way that they create a sense of plasticity and movement for the whole form. Kordis explains that this principle is present throughout iconography, "from the compositional method to the internal organization of the figures, from the manner in which facial features are drawn to movement of the stroke of the brush."[100] Without consistent use of the transverse, we would have figures and images that were stiff and lifeless.

In addition to the transverse principle, Kordis also discusses some other qualities of line in Byzantine iconography. Overall, line is simplified and direct, thus allowing "the purity, lucidity, and freshness even in old faces, in landscapes, or in clothes" to shine through the image.[101] Lines create rhythm and relationships between forms, giving the line "a sense of flow, which is its fundamental characteristic and greatest virtue."[102] Leonid Ouspensky describes this flow as reasonable, consistent; our eye should be able to read and make sense of every line in an icon. "In an icon, everything is logical," he explains, "even the folds of the robe; they underline the shape of the body, they are not lines traced at random, no matter how and no matter where."[103] In an icon, every line counts.

A fluid line is not the same as a curved line. Rather, Byzantine iconography uses a zigzag line, also known as a composite line, to create a sense of fluidity. A composite line takes a curve and breaks it into smaller straight lines. More so than a curved line, a composite line shows the relationships among the forms and is necessary for creating volume and projection in an image. Additionally, the line in Byzantine iconography

---

98. Ibid.
99. Ibid., 8.
100. Ibid., 12.
101. Ibid., 13.
102. Ibid.
103. Ouspensky, *Theology in Color*, 20.

is not a closed line but an open line that gives a sense of moving into the next line, area, or level.[104]

This understanding of line is very helpful for students of iconography as they begin and continue to work on their drawing skills. The tendency is for students to begin by making their lines much too curved and closed. It may seem counterintuitive, but the straight lines convey more movement, life, and relation than a curved line, and that life and relation brings us back to the fundamental understanding of presence and communion within the icon. As one of my iconography teachers frequently says, don't be afraid to use your ruler.

Types of Icons

With an understanding of the basic aesthetical principles of geometry, proportion, line, and color, students are prepared to answer a common question: What makes an image an icon? An icon is not just a picture with a religious theme. An icon is an image that respects and uses the language of Orthodox iconography, a language "rooted in a theology of visual signs, a canon that is understood as the visual expressions of the dogmas of faith."[105] This is the language that was outlined in the above discussion. Additionally, regardless of who is depicted in an icon, the image "is ultimately an image of Jesus Christ, an image of his life, suffering, and resurrection, and of his coming kingdom."[106] The holiness of each saint in an icon is possible because of their relationship with Christ, even when he is not depicted with the saint in a particular icon.

Within the curriculum of the Iconographic Arts Institute, students of iconography are introduced to groupings of icons according to the complexity of their geometry, starting with a simple bust and moving into more complicated icons with multiple figures. Icons may also be grouped according to the kind of story they tell, according to their genre. Sendler uses four basic models or types that he compares to different literary genres. In addition to the Scriptures, genres that serve as the background materials for icons include liturgical texts, hagiography, and the writings of the church fathers. As Sendler explains, the various forms of the icon were influenced by their contemporary literary genres.

104. Kordis, *Icon as Communion*, 16.
105. Yazykova, *Hidden and Triumphant*, 2.
106. Ibid., 19.

In the panegyric model, the details of a saint's life, which are patterned after the life of Christ, surround the image of the saint.[107] Sendler explains that in antiquity, a panegyric speech was a speech given in praise of an important person. However, the panegyric speech also moved beyond mere praise; it was also supposed to move the listeners to actions of their own. As Christian preachers took up this genre, it was applied to the heroic actions of the martyrs and called for equally heroic actions from their listeners. The saint is in the middle of the icon surrounded by smaller figures depicting scenes from his life that make up the frame of the icon. The events are often a reflection of the passion of Christ, his activities during his earthly ministry, or actions from the Beatitudes. For instance, an icon of St. Nicholas shows him visiting prisoners just as Christ asks his followers to do.[108]

In the epic model, the events of a saint's life also surround her image, but the emphasis is more on historical accuracy than exactly mirroring the events from the life of Christ.[109] Both biblical material and the lives of some saints use the epic model.[110] Two examples illustrate this model: icons of the prophet Elijah and icons of the Nativity. Icons of Elijah include Elijah being fed by the crow in the desert, Elijah raising the widow's son, and Elijah crossing the Jordan with Elisha. In the Nativity, the Mother of God is in the middle of the icon, and smaller figures of Saint Joseph, the kings, the angels, and the shepherds circle around her.

The dramatic model depicts a scene of action and tension, such as the Annunciation, the Raising of Lazarus, or the Descent into Hades.[111] Sendler points out that the tensions found in human life and thus the lives of Christ, the Mother of God, and the saints, could be drawn on by iconography just as they could be drawn on for other art forms, including the theater.[112] In an icon, though, the drama points the viewer toward the drama of the redemption of all of humanity. Sendler offers several examples of the tension depicted through the dramatic model. For instance, in the icon of the Crucifixion there is the contrast between the calm of Christ's face and the grief in the faces of the Mother of God and the Beloved Disciple. In the icon of the Annunciation, the Archangel Gabriel sweeps toward the Mother of

---

107. Sendler, *Icon*, 69.
108. Ibid., 70.
109. Ibid.
110. Ibid., 72.
111. Ibid., 73.
112. Ibid., 72.

God, his feet, arm, and wings all caught in motion as he approaches her while the Mother of God is seated quietly on her throne.[113]

The theological treatise is the fourth model. "If theology deepens a truth by intellectual reasoning," explains Sendler, "the image [of the theological model] offers us truth as a vision."[114] In this respect, all icons are theological treatises. However, more than the other models, the model of the theological treatise is more figurative than literal. Sendler points out that particularly in Russia starting in the sixteenth century, "the theological meaning itself became the direct subject of the icons: they were no longer a personal presence of the prototype but a treatise on theology."[115] Sendler uses Rublev's Trinity to explain this model. The Byzantine version of this icon, based on the eighteenth chapter of Genesis and the understanding of the three strangers as the Trinity approaching Abraham, was titled the Hospitality of Abraham. In the translations of this icon that came before Rublev, three visitors, the three angels, were clearly depicted, but the icon also included a table set with various objects, a servant killing the calf to provide the meal for the guests, and Abraham and Sarah serving the guests. In Rublev's Trinity, however, these historical elements are removed or minimized, and "the only remaining element was the three heavenly visitors, in silent conversation; and the table became an altar having only a Eucharistic cup on it."[116] The other elements that remained, such as the tree and rock, also became more symbolic than historical. For Sendler, these theological icons are not read as easily as the other models. He seems to regret the development of this model, despite the beauty and harmony of some of the examples, because it seems to focus more on the intellectual abilities of the painter and the viewer than on the icon as a manifestation of the mystery of Christ and his Incarnation.[117]

The Iconoclast Controversy

The whole history of the Eastern Church lies open to a new student of iconography, especially since Western Christians are generally less familiar with the history of Byzantium than with that of the West. For Catholic

113. Ibid., 73.
114. Ibid.
115. Ibid., 74.
116. Ibid., 75.
117. Ibid.

seminarians and other students of the icon, the iconoclast controversy is one of the primary threads in that history. The controversy has a large scope, and it is "unlikely that the issues can be neatly categorized."[118] Scholars describe the iconoclast controversy in terms of politics and theology, the secular and the sacred. This description of the controversy will use broad strokes to discuss the major events that took place and the arguments on each side of the controversy.

Overview of the Iconoclast Controversy

By 730 the emperor Leo III issued an edict against icons, and Constantine V, his son, called the Council of Hieria in 754. This council stated that the painting and venerating of icons was idolatrous. According to this council, icons of Christ were heretical because it is impossible to represent God. It was also claimed that icons misrepresent Christ because they "either separate his humanity and divinity or confuse them."[119] The decrees of Hieria were reversed by Nicaea II. However, iconoclasm became an issue again under Leo V, thus starting the second stage of iconoclasm that continued until 843. The controversy ended with a synodal decree by Partiarch Methodios. This was followed by a public procession to Hagia Sophia and the declaration of the Triumph of Orthodoxy, which continues to be celebrated by Orthodox Christians around the world each year on the first Sunday of Lent.[120] Generally speaking, members of the military were iconoclasts and monks were the strongest defenders of the icon. The polarization is one reason for the bitterness of the controversy and the extent of the physical damage that resulted from it.

The materials of the historical record for the iconoclast controversy were shaped by geography and the outcome of the controversy. Archaeological evidence indicates figurative mosaic icons were removed in Constantinople and in other areas, and from 730 to 787 and from 813 to 843 the production of figurative icons ceased in Constantinople as well.[121] Locations far from Constantinople, such as the Monastery of St. Catherine in Sinai, did not experience much destruction of icons. Most of the literature that we have now from the iconoclast period that describes the controversy is weighted

118. Cormack, "Art and Iconoclasm," 751.
119. Ibid.
120. Ibid.
121. Ibid., 752.

toward the iconophiles since much of the literature of the iconoclasts was destroyed when the controversy concluded. Their arguments must be rebuilt through the work of the iconophiles, and "the acts of the Seventh Ecumenical Council (Nicaea II)" that "are the best source of information on the subject."[122] The council will be discussed more below.

Scholars of Byzantium usually cite two primary causes of iconoclasm, one from within Christianity and one from outside forces. The first cause addresses the possible underlying opposition to representative art in Christianity from its beginning. Scholars focusing on this cause have looked at the support for and opposition to icons beginning in early Christianity but see that "neither side [was] formulating a consistent position."[123] As the production and use of icons became more popular, the need for a theory and theology of the image became more pressing. Developments such as canon 82 of Quinisext Council in 680–681, which states that Christ should be represented as a man rather than as a lamb, may have exacerbated or provoked the iconoclasts.

The causes from outside forces involve the political circumstances of the eighth century and other challenges faced by the Byzantine Empire. The military pressures of the Arabs, the religious pressures of Islam, and natural disasters led political leaders to look for a scapegoat, which led them to the production and veneration of icons.[124] When iconoclasm became a policy of the imperial leaders, both iconophiles and iconoclasts had good reason to develop their arguments as fully as possible. The iconoclasts equated heresy with icons and "on the other side the nature of orthodoxy was defined to include the icon."[125] The iconoclasts cited the second commandment against graven images; the iconophiles argued that this commandment was altered by the Incarnation and the practices of the early church. All of this developed into a period "which is distinctive for the vehemence and sophistication of its rhetoric."[126] Because the iconoclasts and the iconophiles shared some important understandings, perhaps they needed the strong rhetoric to differentiate one position from the other.

---

122. Sahas, *Icon and Logos*, x.
123. Cormack, "Art and Iconoclasm," 753.
124. Ibid., 754.
125. Ibid.
126. Ibid.

Arguments of the Iconoclasts and Iconophiles

Jaroslav Pelikan provides an excellent summary of the two points of view within the iconoclastic controversy, the ways in which the two sides agreed with each other and where they diverged. Both the iconoclasts and the iconophiles agreed that Christ was truly present in the Eucharist; the difficulty arose when they discussed whether or how the sacramental principle could be applied to materials other than the Eucharist.[127] They both had a pastoral concern for the people, particularly the uneducated and illiterate. The iconoclasts thought images led the uneducated into idolatry, while the iconophiles thought images could replace the written texts the uneducated could not access.[128] Belief in Christ in the Eucharist and concern for the people are, of course, extremely important. These commonalities demonstrate that both sides were coming from within the Christian world, from a place of faith.

The two sides shared some agreement about the concept of images as well. They agreed this concept was helpful because of the Genesis account of humanity's creation in God's image.[129] Additionally, both sides agreed that "Christ is the image of the Father in a special way," yet for the iconoclasts it did not necessarily follow that Christ could therefore be depicted or circumscribed.[130] In addition to their agreement concerning the scriptural basis for the concept of images, both sides could also cite apostolic and patristic sources to support their arguments. Pelikan explains that because the iconoclasts used legitimate texts, we can see "the ambiguity of the tradition and hence the argument from tradition."[131] The doctrine of both the iconophiles and the iconoclasts was in development, and eventually that development would clarify the place images have in Christian theology and spirituality.

Even though it was during the eighth and ninth centuries that the doctrinal arguments against icons developed, Christianity always had some iconoclast tendencies. Pelikan notes that the role of Exodus 20:4 in their arguments explains that all "five of our major orthodox sources from the eighth and ninth centuries—John of Damascus, John of Jerusalem, the

---

127. Pelikan, "Images of the Invisible," 94.
128. Ibid., 95.
129. Ibid.
130. Ibid., 96.
131. Ibid., 102–3.

Second Council of Nicaea, Theodore of Studios, and Nicephorus—took the trouble to note the iconoclast exegesis of this disturbing passage and to refute it."[132] The iconoclasts essentially understood that for an image to be a true image, it had to be identical in essence with its source, as the Son is with the Father. Thus, any pictorial representation of Christ must be a false image. The only true image of Christ could be the Eucharist because it is the essence of Christ. The only exception the iconoclasts would make to this stance was the image of the cross.[133] For the iconophiles, this exception was an inconsistency in the arguments of the iconoclasts.

For the iconoclasts, the iconophiles threatened the defense of the Trinity that had been accomplished by the church fathers. The doctrine of the Trinity was legitimate on the grounds that worship was directed to one God, not three gods or other figures that were worshiped as well. To the iconoclasts, defense of the Trinity was much more difficult if it appeared that "the worship of the orthodox was addressed to a plurality of objects."[134] According to the iconoclasts, icons divided the two natures of Christ, his divine nature that could not be depicted and his human nature that could be depicted, and the Council of Chalcedon had defined Christ's two natures as inseparable.[135]

In some respects, the conflict between the iconophiles and the iconoclasts came down to different definitions of an image. The iconophiles said that "an image had to be understood and defined on the basis of that to which it was related."[136] Rather than an image existing on its own, an image is intimately related to its prototype so that any reverence given to the image is passed on to that prototype. The iconophiles developed this understanding of the relationship between the image and its prototype into an understanding of the universe as a hierarchy of images with a "close relation and a creative involvement between the image and its prototype."[137] A freestanding image with some kind of power of its own and that therefore could become an idol could not be a part of this scheme.

The iconophiles pointed out that icons resonate with healthy human psychology because people naturally use objects and pictures to remind

132. Ibid., 107.
133. Ibid., 110.
134. Ibid., 114.
135. Ibid., 116.
136. Ibid., 119.
137. Ibid., 120.

them of their loved ones. Through this normal and loving use of images, a person's sense of sight is sanctified: "The icon served as a means for this hallowing of sight, combined as it was with the hearing of the word."[138] Through this argument, the iconophiles affirmed the body as a channel for salvation; the body, including the sense of sight, should in no way be despised because not only did God make it good in the first place, but he also uses it to bring us back into communion with him. When the sense of sight was directed toward holy images, they saw the icon could be a way to resist idolatry, the worship of false images. This point hinges on to what a given image is dedicated; icons are devoted to God while heathen images were devoted to other deities or more evil forces.[139] As they make this distinction, the iconophiles also distinguish between the worship due to God alone and the veneration given to holy objects such as icons, the Gospel book, and vessels of the altar.[140]

As with the iconoclasts, the iconophiles built their arguments on the Old Testament Scriptures, though they emphasized Moses building the tabernacle more than the second commandment. In this way, the iconophiles claimed the biblical tradition for themselves rather than leaving the portions of the Old Testament that address images and materials to the arguments of the iconoclasts. The iconoclasts also affirmed the practice of "reinterpreting the law of the Old Testament in the light of the incarnation taught in the New Testament," and by doing so affirmed the primary Christian stance of reading and interpreting every part of the Scriptures through the lens of Christ.[141]

The most significant argument of the iconophiles is rooted in the Incarnation and that Christ is one person with two natures, fully human and fully divine. In the Old Testament, images of God were forbidden because God was not incarnate, but with the Incarnation of Christ, humanity now has an image of God. The people of his time could physically experience him just as they could any other man or woman.[142] Christ was naturally circumscribed because of his human body. We do not even expect that a picture of an ordinary person will portray or contain all that he or she is.[143]

138. Ibid., 122.
139. Ibid.
140. Ibid., 127.
141. Ibid., 125.
142. Ibid., 128.
143. Ibid., 130.

The iconophiles understood that matter, and thus the Incarnation, was beautiful and good. The iconoclasts may have thought they were protecting the dignity of Christ's divinity, but "it was not true loyalty to him to seek to protect him from the limitation and circumscription of a genuinely human body."[144] The iconophiles understood that the living and historical reality of the human life and experience of Christ, "the places he went, the objects he touched, the people who saw, heard, and touched him," was at stake in the iconoclast controversies.[145] They also countered the arguments of the iconoclasts regarding the Trinity. Those who venerated icons were not dividing their veneration among different gods or even the different persons within the Trinity. Rather, "there is only one mode of worship, whether addressed to the entire Trinity because of the unity of nature or to the icon of Christ because of the unity of hypostasis."[146] The iconophiles maintained Christ's humanity and the oneness of God in relation to sacred images.

Essentially, the iconophiles argued that the gospel hinges on an Incarnate God since only a truly human Christ could be humanity's salvation and that the doctrine of the Incarnation and that of the icon could not be separated. To reject the icon is to reject the gospel.[147] The icon was and is a constant reminder of the reality of the Incarnation and a physical path through which we can offer our worship to the Father, the Son, and the Holy Spirit.

Definition of the Seventh Ecumenical Council

Norman J. Tanner, the editor of an English translation of the canons of Nicaea II, serves as our source for discussion of Nicaea II. The council brought clarity and some closure to the iconoclast controversies as it declared null and void the Council of Hieria of 754.[148] It took a number of years for the council to gather, and looking at some of the details of how the gathering occurred may give us an additional appreciation for the perseverance it took to resolve the controversy. Patriarch Paul IV of Constantinople asked Empress Irene to call an ecumenical council in order to address the iconoclast controversy and other decrees passed by the Council of Hieria. Prior to the council, Partriarch Paul IV was succeeded by Patriarch Tarasius. Pope

---

144. Ibid., 128.
145. Ibid., 131.
146. Ibid., 129.
147. Ibid., 132.
148. Tanner, *Decrees*, 131.

Hadrian I was called to the council by Irene and Constantine VI, for whom she was the regent since he was still a minor, and the patriarch sent the same letter to the three other eastern patriarchs. Pope Hadrian approved the gathering of the council and sent two legates.[149] It was not easy for this council to be held in the first place since its first meeting in August of 786 was disrupted by iconoclast soldiers and had to be reassembled in Nicaea in 787, with the recall of the papal legates.

During the second session of the council "the cult of sacred images as explained in the letters of Pope Hadrian I . . . were read out."[150] In the definition of the council, the inflammatory language was used in reference to iconoclast bishops. According to the definition, these bishops "followed unholy men and trusting in their own frenzies they calumniated the holy church, which Christ our God has espoused to himself, and *they failed to distinguish the holy from the profane,* asserting that the icons of our Lord and of his saints were no different from the wood of satanic idols" (italics in original).[151] The council also included three anathemas that apply to holy images, essential teachings that a person must confirm if he believes in the Incarnation and has a proper understanding of holy images. If a person does not confess that the humanity of Christ can be represented, if a person does not find the representation of evangelical scenes acceptable, and if a person does not accept that the representations named in the first two anathemas "as standing for the Lord and his saints," he will be anathema.[152] The ninth canon of the council explains how to deal with the materials generated by the iconoclasts. It also gives another example of the strong rhetoric the fathers used against the iconoclasts: "All those childish baubles and bacchic rantings, the false writings composed against the venerable icons, should be given in at the Episcopal building in Constantinople, so that they can be put away with the other heretical books."[153] Those who hid the iconoclast writings were to be suspended or excommunicated.

The council fathers affirmed all of the teachings of the previous ecumenical councils that support the arguments of the iconophiles. The council proclaimed that the use of representational art is not an innovation but is "in harmony with the history of the spread of the gospel, as it provides

---

149. Ibid.
150. Ibid.
151. Ibid., 134.
152. Ibid., 137.
153. Ibid., 146.

confirmation that the becoming of the Word of God was real and not just imaginary, and as it brings us a similar benefit."[154] After explaining that images of Christ, the Mother of God, the angels, and the saints made from a variety of appropriate materials should be displayed in churches, homes, and other public spaces, the council carefully differentiates between the veneration given to a holy image and the adoration given to God:

> Certainly this is not the full adoration in accordance with our faith, which is properly paid only to the divine nature, but it resembles that given to the figure of the honoured and life-giving cross, and also to the holy books of the gospels and to other sacred cult objects. . . . Indeed, the honor paid to an image traverses it, reaching the model; and he who venerates the image, venerates the person represented in that image.[155]

Those who work for the creation and veneration of images in our contemporary times have much of the support they need from the Seventh Ecumenical Council. While that support may need to be put into contemporary wording, the explanations for some of the questions that may be asked today have already been made by our predecessors in the church.

In the final chapter of his book *Images of the Divine: The Theology of Icons at the Seventh Ecumenical Council*, Ambrosios Giakalis discusses the significance of the work of Nicaea II. It was essentially a christological council that was sorting through the Christologies of the iconoclasts and the iconophiles. For the iconoclasts, images became blasphemous idols because they took the grace of Christ and inserted it into a dead object; for the iconophiles, denying the grace at work in an icon was paramount to denying the Incarnation. Giakalis describes the iconoclast controversy as "the last phase of the formation of the Christological doctrine of the undivided catholic Church."[156] The different Christologies resulted in different attitudes toward matter, with the iconoclasts regarding the distance between the material and the spiritual as too great to be "bridged by any sanctified matter apart from the Eucharistic body of Christ." The iconophiles, on the other hand, saw matter as "a channel of communication with the divine; it could offer access to God to the ordinary faithful."[157] The iconophiles had a much more hopeful view of the material world.

154. Ibid., 134.
155. Ibid., 136.
156. Giakalis, *Images of the Divine*, 130.
157. Ibid., 137.

In Giakalis's analysis, the most essential difference between the iconophiles and the iconoclasts was their different understandings of the uncreated energies of the Holy Trinity. The iconoclasts saw the energy of God as completely confined to God himself. This preserved a sense of God's complete transcendence but kept his energy removed from the people. On the other hand, the iconophiles, with their understanding of the created and uncreated energies of God, could say that God was completely holy by nature as well as present in "every human saint as a deifying energy and in the saint's image as a sanctifying energy."[158] Through his created energies, God bridged the space between humanity and himself.

For the purposes of this book and its practical applications, Giakalis's discussion of the icon as an agent of truth is particularly helpful. The icon as an agent of truth is part of the understanding of education as a cultural ideal that grew out of the Seventh Ecumenical Council and the stance of the iconophiles. This stance built on the practice and value of lifelong learning:

> This work is not a matter of studying in a school for a short time and following a course of studies which inevitably comes to an end. It becomes a manner of life, a mode of existence, and one grows old always learning and never graduating from the believing community of the Church.[159]

This lifelong learning built on learning through sight, through the icon, the depths of which are infinite. The ecclesiastical training and learning done through the icon incorporated people into the church, that body "of people saved and sanctified by God."[160] The visual image is a manner of education available to the highly educated as well as those who have not had such opportunities, and through respect for the iconographic canon, it is as stable as the Scriptures.

The opposition of the iconoclasts forced the iconophiles to define what they thought and believed about sacred images. The iconophile writers developed a theory of images that is built on three fundamental points: Christ serves as the image of the Father, humanity serves as an image of Christ, and the icon serves as "the artistic image of Christ and the saints."[161] This theory fits with the model of the church as sacrament with Christ as the sacrament of the Father and the church as a sacrament of Christ, a model to

---

158. Ibid.
159. Ibid., 53.
160. Ibid.
161. Cormack, "Art and Iconoclasm," 755.

which we can add the icon serving as a sacrament of each of the prototypes depicted. Because of the iconoclast controversy, "icons became a defining feature of the Orthodox church,"[162] and a rich tradition was defended and further developed, a tradition that we have the privilege of becoming a part of in our own place and time.

Treatise III of *On the Divine Images*: A Summary and Response

In this section, I will discuss one example from the church fathers who defended the icon by developing the arguments in support of the iconophiles. I drew the pattern for this discussion from my course in theological anthropology at Mount Angel Seminary with Dr. Katy Leamy, and I would use a similar pattern for an assignment for seminary students, such as in an elective course in iconography or a course on the theology of art. This assignment would be about the same length as my summary and response here. Summarizing the material gives the students the opportunity to demonstrate they have understood it and to work on the essential skills of paraphrasing and integrating quotations into their text. The analysis of the anthropological assumptions of the text and its pastoral applications helps the seminarians build critical thinking and apply the material to their current field education assignments and future pastoral work.

John, a monk of Damascus, drew on the church fathers who preceded him and laid the foundation for a theology of the icon. According to John, in order to defend the icon we must respect the tradition by reading Scripture intelligently, absorbing the teaching of the fathers, and respecting the physical as well as spiritual aspects of our own existence; understand the nature of the icon; and understand the nature of veneration. Because he lived outside of the Byzantine Empire during the iconoclast controversy, John could be more forthright and outspoken than some of his contemporaries.[163] *On the Divine Images* is composed of three treatises that are essentially the same treatise written and revised on three different occasions. The third treatise also has a *florilegium*, a collection of passages from church fathers who also wrote on the icon or discussed it as a part of a larger work. This summary and response will focus on the text of the third treatise.

---

162. Ibid.
163. John of Damascus, *On the Divine Images*, 9.

In the first section, John explains that iconoclasm is "a ruse of the devil,"[164] who does not want humanity to understand its potential for deification. The devil will distract and confuse humanity through the misuse of words so that humanity will neglect and abuse the icon. Fortunately, John explains, humanity may avoid these traps by adhering to the teaching he offers in his treatise. John's most important teaching in the first section concerns reading the Scriptures, particularly the passages concerning Moses. "It is good to search the Scriptures," he explains, "but take care to do it with discretion."[165] John explains that while in the Old Testament God forbids the making of images of himself or other gods, he did so because the Israelites were falling into idolatry and because God had not yet become incarnate. God issued this portion of the law so that "one should not worship, or offer the veneration of worship, to creation instead of the Creator, but only to the One who fashioned all."[166] Worship is due to God alone, and when the circumstances made abiding by that truth difficult for the Israelites, God gave the law to make it easier, even if people chose to disobey it.

John's second and third points in his third treatise build on the first. He explains that while some of the most important theological words and concepts, such as "the name of the Trinity or *homoousion* or one nature of the divinity" do not appear in the Scriptures, the church fathers still base their development of these words and concepts in the Scriptures.[167] In the next paragraph he explains that with the revelation of Christ, God reaches for his people through physical reality "so through bodily vision we come to spiritual contemplation."[168] With the Incarnation, people are able to meet God face to face.

In the next two sections, which compose the majority of the third treatise, John explains the nature of the icon and the nature of veneration. He uses a series of questions to move succinctly through these sections. First, he explains that an image is "a likeness and pattern and impression" of the archetype that should not be equated with the archetype, and that the purpose of an image is to guide us to spiritual realities for the sake of our salvation.[169]

---

164. Ibid., 82.
165. Ibid., 83.
166. Ibid., 87.
167. Ibid., 92.
168. Ibid., 93.
169. Ibid., 96.

Next, John discusses types of images. The first type, the Son who is the image of the Father, is the basis for all of the other types of images. The next types are God's thought about what he will bring about through his will and humanity as an image of God. John reminds his readers that God himself is the first maker of an image, the image of his Son, and that God did this so that humanity could be in communion with him.[170]

Several of the types of images involve Scripture. The Scriptures describe images or forms that give humanity some understanding of invisible beings such as angels and demons. The Scriptures have images in the Old Testament that prefigure what is to come in the New Testament, such as the burning bush prefiguring the Mother of God.[171] The last types of images John discusses are those portrayed through words in books and forms we receive though our sight that "record the images of virtuous men of the past for emulation and remembrance and to arouse our zeal."[172] The ultimate purpose of these images is communion with God, with Christ, and with his saints.

John follows his explanation of images with a definition of veneration as "a sign of submission, that of subordination and humility."[173] He explains that the first type of veneration, which people today would call worship, is due to God alone because he "alone is venerable by nature" and should receive that veneration simply because he is.[174] Other types of veneration due to God include that of wonder at God, thanksgiving for the gifts God has given us, hope that he will respond to our needs, and repentance for our sins. We also offer veneration to various creatures, but even this veneration should lead us back to God. We venerate the saints; places and objects of the Old Testament because of their place in salvation history; objects dedicated to God such as the Gospel book, icons, and the utensils of the altar; and visions of the prophets that portray realities to come.

The last categories address the veneration of people, beginning with the veneration that applies to everyone, the veneration of "one another as having a portion of God and having come to be in the image of God."[175] People also offer veneration to rulers and other authorities, and the needy

170. Ibid., 101.
171. Ibid., 99.
172. Ibid., 100.
173. Ibid., 104.
174. Ibid.
175. Ibid., 109.

offer it to those who help them. Even with these categories, though, John implores his readers to understand that pure veneration is offered to God alone, and "to all others what is due is reckoned for the Lord's sake."[176] Essentially, the faithful must keep their perspective when they offer veneration of any kind so that they do not venerate the matter of which the image is made but that which the matter depicts.

Anthropological Presuppositions

Several assumptions underlie John's points. First, he assumes that human beings have a fundamental need for or orientation toward veneration. Even in the course of everyday events, people can and should recognize those who have assisted them and be grateful for that assistance. Second, he assumes that images are a fundamental part of how the world works and how God works. God reaches for us and we reach for God through a system of beautiful and profound images. Forgetting or neglecting this point can lead to gnostic thinking or the denial of, at various levels, the reality and consequences of the Incarnation.

Analysis and Response

The first part of John's treatise in which he defends tradition and the icon reflects several aspects of the theology curriculum of Mount Angel Seminary and the good formation of our students. First, his emphasis on the need for a sound understanding of the Scriptures echoes the approach of our own Scripture courses. It isn't enough to know the content; we must also know how to read them intelligently through a christological key. Second, his discussion of the Incarnation fits with our Christology courses, and his emphasis on the respect for our own physical nature builds on this point. This can encourage our students to acknowledge the ways in which God reaches us through our physical experience, including but of course not limited to our encounters with iconography. Text-based study is important, but so is the education we receive through the images around us. Third, John's description of iconoclasm as a "ruse of the devil" reminds us that struggles with evil can be a reality, perhaps particularly when we are approaching a better understanding of a concept as fundamental as the

---

176. Ibid., 110.

role and power of sacred images. I have spoken about this with my fellow students of the icon on numerous occasions, and I continue to recognize it in my own experience.

John's point concerning images as a fundamental part of God's nature can help us respect the power and pervasiveness that images have in our lives and help us to be mindful about adhering to good practices in terms of our own use and viewing of images. This applies to our day-to-day living, such as our reading material and the videos we see; it is equally important as I introduce students to the study of iconography. They need to learn what constitutes a good and prayerful icon, to be able to discern the difference between a sound image and an image that does not respect the canon. They need to understand that the ultimate measure of an icon is whether the viewer can truly pray with it and that the aesthetics play an important part in that experience. When they learn to be discerning and thoughtful about the icons they select for their own prayer and for their future ministries, they are respecting the power and the pervasiveness of images in all our lives.

Pastoral Applicability

Since the first two of John's treatises are essentially contained in the third, I would assign just the third treatise as part of the reading for an elective in iconography. It is a manageable piece of reading in terms of its length, and the *florilegia* may also support some of the work I've done with students and commonplace books. John's clarity may also make his explanations more accessible than some of the other materials about iconography that are currently available. Given the range of language abilities and experience and given that an elective in iconography would most likely be open to college as well as graduate students, John's third treatise could be very suitable and appropriate.

Because of its clear outline, this is also a text seminarians can easily use in their current pastoral placements and future ministries. John clearly defines veneration and repeatedly emphasizes that all of the types of veneration that he describes are good so long as they are directed toward love and respect for God. This may help priests and pastors answer the questions of their parishioners about icons or other practices that involve images. At the conclusion of this summary and response, my main question is how a more explicit or concentrated focus on images within our theological studies can deepen those studies, our pastoral ministries, and all the ways in which we care for and nurture the spiritual lives of others, as well as our own communal and personal prayer.

The Icon in Twentieth-Century Russia

At times, the study of iconography can feel rather ephemeral. We will never know the identity of the painters of many of our ancient prototypes. Our prototypes may also have originated in areas of the world with which we have been, until now, relatively unfamiliar. As seminarians and other students of the icon discern how the icon will become a part of their lives, it may be helpful to take in the stories of our predecessors whose names we do have, particularly those whose perseverance has made our own studies possible. Regardless of the place the icon eventually has in a student's life, learning about the icon in twentieth-century Russia will give her the opportunity to meet some of her predecessors, to experience this particular corner of the communion of saints. The story of the icon in Russia in the twentieth century is a story of faith, sacrifice, and redemption, a defense of the Incarnation and reality of the love of God brought to humanity through Jesus Christ.

After the conversion of Russia to Christianity in 980, many Byzantine iconographers, clergy, and other liturgical artists worked in Russia and influenced its liturgical art and worship. As Russia developed its own iconographic styles and schools, some of the figures were simplified and iconographers focused on panel icons, since Russian churches were made of wood, which is less conducive to mosaics and frescos than stone. Additionally, because of the high icon screens in Russian churches, the icons were further away from the viewers. To compensate, iconographers used bolder and brighter colors that gave more emphasis to the silhouettes of the figures.[177]

The first period of Russian iconography lasted from the tenth to approximately the first third of the thirteenth century. During this time the Byzantine influence was the greatest on the Russian icon. Schools developed in Vladimir, Novgorod, and other cities. In her discussion of the iconography tradition prior to the traumatic events of the twentieth century, Irina Yazykova explains that "today's icon painters are still the direct heirs of the

---

177. Hart, *Techniques*, 16.

master iconographers of ancient Rus.'"[178] The second period, the rest of the thirteenth and the fourteenth century, was overshadowed by the Tartars. Because Novgorod and Pskov remained free of the Tartars, their schools of iconography were able to continue to develop. During the fifteenth century, Moscow was the primary center for iconography; at this time the Tartars were expelled and Russia was united.[179]

After the sixteenth century, Russian iconography became degraded or debased. More naturalistic figures were used, and the icons often violated the principle of keeping the secondary elements at the service of the primary figures. These practices obscured the theological purpose of the icon. During the nineteenth century, scientific developments enabled the ancient icons to be cleaned and analyzed anew. This work removed layers of dirt and soot embedded in the varnishes that covered the painting, revealing the beauty and harmony hidden below.[180]

One of the finest books on the history of iconography that has been published in recent years is Irina Yazykova's *Hidden and Triumphant: The Underground Struggle to Save Russian Iconography*. Her book not only tells this important story, but it also contains one of the best short introductions to the icon that I have found thus far. In this section I will focus on two points from her book that help to illustrate the connections between the Russian iconographers and those of us who are students of the icon today. First is the rediscovery of the icon in Russia that coincided with the Russian Revolution. This is followed by the story of the Russian emigration after the revolution that built on that rediscovery and helped to bring the icon to the rest of the world, including the Iconographic Arts Institute.

The title of the third chapter of *Hidden and Triumphant*, "The Discovery of the Icon and the New Iconoclasts," points toward the central irony of Yazykova's story. Just as the Bolsheviks were gaining power, the true light and beauty of the medieval Russian icon was being uncovered. As death, torture, and mistrust overtook so many, another instrument that speaks of God's love and freedom was being given back to the world. Conservationists were removing centuries of varnish, dirt, and badly executed restoration efforts. Yazykova explains that in the final years of tsarist Russia, the beauty and joy of these icons led both intellectuals and ordinary people to conclude "that the past as a whole would have to be

---

178. Yazykova, *Hidden and Triumphant*, 27.
179. Hart, *Techniques*, 17.
180. Ibid.

reassessed."[181] Given the events that were coming, though, the icon also stood as a vision of the truth and goodness of God in a time of great darkness. Additionally, even though in the early twentieth century the intellectuals were moving away from an interest in the icon, the common people maintained their popular devotions to them, even if their understanding of the meaning of the icon had become obscured.

The rediscovery of the icon included much more than a greater understanding of the icon as a physical object; it also "relates, in fact, to a whole series of scientific and scholarly discoveries."[182] The areas involved include archaeology, history, the restoration arts, philology, and theology. Essentially, the whole context from which the Russian icon had grown was rediscovered along with dozens of important icons from the medieval period, including Andrei Rublev's Holy Trinity.[183] These discoveries resulted in an exhibit of ancient icons in Moscow in 1907, followed by a larger exhibit in 1913. As the icons were restored and the craft of iconography was rediscovered, Russian theologians and philosophers were also rediscovering the theology and profound language of the icon. The scholars affirmed that knowledge of history, liturgy, and theology, particularly the church fathers, was key to understanding iconography. The icon "brought back to the Church the creative spirit of the church fathers and served to counteract the spirit of perfunctory ritualism and hypocritical dogmatism characteristic of the Synodal period."[184] The rediscovery of the icon blossomed into a renewal of theology as a whole.

The rediscovery and renewal of the icon was swept into the devastating iconoclasm of the Communist government in Russia. Human lives, icons, and the theology that explained the true life and destiny of the human person were attacked and destroyed. Yazykova explains the suffering of most iconographers and artists:

> For some the price they paid was exile and forced emigration. Others abandoned icon painting and took up another craft. Not infrequently, they died of starvation. Still others were left to rot in the Soviet gulag. It is not for nothing that the icon has always been called a "window into another world." The closure of that window made it all the harder to catch a glimpse of the light from this other

---

181. Yazykova, *Hidden and Triumphant*, 46.
182. Ibid., 51.
183. Ibid., 54.
184. Ibid., 55.

world—the light from the kingdom of heaven that inspires people to stand in the light and resist the darkness.[185]

Yet people were still able to catch that glimpse of the light from God. Even as political events brought tragedy and death, people still caught the light and kept moving toward it, both those who remained in Russia and those who went into exile.

Eugene Trubetskoi, one of the philosophers who worked on the rediscovery of the iconographic tradition at the beginning of the twentieth century, wrote his book *Icons: Theology in Color* in 1915. Trubetskoi speaks to the tension between the outward pain and horror of that time and the hoped-for graces of the icon. He wrote:

> We need these glad tidings of spring and the red dawn that heralds the joy of sunrise. So as not to fall into the despondency but fight to the end, we need to carry before us the banner on which the beauty of heaven is joined with the sunny visage of the glorified *holy* Russia. May the benediction inherited from our distant forebearers be an appeal to creative work. May it augur a new great period in our history.[186]

That blessing did bring forth new life for the icon, and each student of the Iconographic Arts Institute and each of my students who study the icon through Mount Angel Seminary are recipients of that blessing, love, and sacrifice.

The story of those who remained in Russia is important, yet for the purposes of this book, the focus here is on those who went into exile, since it is primarily through their work that I have been introduced to the iconographic tradition. With the 1917 revolution, the Bolsheviks attempted to build a new culture in Russia, one disassociated from the centuries of Christian history that preceded them, and those who resisted the new culture suffered many forms of persecution. Many artists, philosophers, theologians, and clergy fled Russia, and while "they were deprived of their native land," explains Irina Yazykova, they were not "deprived of their personal culture, because they were not only bearers of culture but also creators of culture."[187] The best example is the Parisian theological school that developed many strands of theology, including iconography. Essentially, as the exiles settled

---

185. Ibid., 65.
186. Trubetskoi, *Icons*, 70.
187. Yazykova, *Hidden and Triumphant*, 67.

in their new homes, they built and decorated churches, and through that work they revived the Russian iconographic tradition.

Dmitry Semyonovich Stelletsky initiated much of this work. He was an artist and antique collector, and even before he left Russia he wanted to establish a new artistic movement grounded in medieval Russia. He left in 1910 and began working in France, where he completed many icons, including an icon entitled "The Assembly of the New Russian Martyrs Killed by the Godless Ones" that "became the prototype for many subsequent works on this theme, which, sadly, gained ever-increasing relevance throughout the twentieth century."[188] The most well known of his works are the frescos and iconostasis at the Church of Saint Sergius in Paris, the church that served as the center for Russian immigrants in the city, and where Sergei Bulgakov founded the Saint Sergius Orthodox Theological School.

Another notable member of the community of Saint Sergius, Sister Joanna Reitlinger, was particularly notable because prior to the twentieth century, Russian Orthodoxy had very few women iconographers. Women had often executed needlework patterns for vestments and other church linens, but in the twentieth century women designed icons and mastered the whole profession from miniatures to monumental work. The life of Sister Joanna "exemplifies in miniature the paths trodden by Russia's Orthodox intelligentsia during the twentieth century."[189] In 1924 she followed her spiritual director, Sergei Bulgakov, to Paris, helped him found the Saint Sergius Orthodox Theological School, and established her atelier in the attic of the Church of Saint Serigus. Her theological discussions with Bulgakov also led him to write his important book, *The Icon and Its Veneration*. Sister Joanna particularly focused on monumentalism, and she frescoed churches in France, England, and Czechoslovakia. On his deathbed, Father Bulgakov urged her to return to Russia, and in 1955 she was able to do so. Through the help of close friends, she was able to continue with iconography and bring the tradition she had helped to rediscover back to her homeland.

After World War I, the number of iconographers leaving Russia increased, including the monk Gregory Kroug, who became a teacher of Leonid Ouspensky. After Kroug left Russia for France in 1931, he spent time in a psychiatric hospital. He was taken from the hospital by his spiritual father, Father Sergei Shevich. Father Shevich took Kroug to his monastery, and he was tonsured in 1948. Eventually he lived in the Hermitage

---

188. Ibid., 69.
189. Ibid., 72.

of the Holy Spirit in Le Mesnil Saint-Denis for twenty years. He did work for churches in France, England, and Holland, and he created frescoes in the Church of the Three Hierarchs in Paris with Leonid Ouspensky. Kroug is particularly known for his willingness to experiment, and "this avoidance of imitation distinguishes him from other émigré iconographers. His experience of tradition and the canon was very much a living thing—something that touched his very core."[190] Unfortunately, because of his experimental processes and because his experience as an émigré made it difficult to follow the entire traditional process of creating an icon, some of his works have deteriorated.

The renewal worked through the Russian émigrés in the West included not just iconography but the whole of Orthodox theology. Theologians who contributed to this renewal include Father Sergei Bulgakov, Father George Florovsky, Father Alexander Schmemann, Father John Meyendorff, Paul Evdokimov, Metropolitan Anthony Bloom, and many others. Through this renewal, additional theologians contributed to the scholarly study of iconography. Leonid Ouspensky, with his book *Theology of the Icon*, which was first published in French in 1960 and has since been translated into ten languages, became one of the most prominent scholars in this area. Because of his work, explains Yazykova, "icon painting has been firmly established among iconographers as a branch of theology, and the canon as the foundation of iconography."[191] It is my hope that through the projects described in the third section of this book that at least a small portion of the iconographical and theological work of the Russian émigrés may be offered to Catholic seminarians, including my own students at Mount Angel Seminary.

The Life of Leonid Ouspensky

Leonid Ouspensky, iconographer, scholar, and teacher, was one of the many Russians who fled Russia in the early twentieth century and regrouped in Paris. As we have seen above, he was a student of Gregory Kroug and a teacher of Patrick Doolan. Through recent publication of several books pertaining to his work, those of us studying iconography in the West may learn more of Ouspensky's story. He was born in 1902 in the Voronezh region of Russia; his parents later had two more daughters. He attended school and

190. Ibid., 83.
191. Ibid., 85.

worked with his father on his estate until 1917, at which point he began to participate in the atheistic activities of his peers. He preached atheism and physically disrespected many icons. As a teenager he tried to enlist in the Red Army several times before he was accepted in 1918.[192]

During his time in the army he was part of the Zhloba Calvary Division; by 1920 Ouspensky was one of just a few dozen survivors from eight thousand men. He was captured by the White Army and immediately condemned to death by firing squad. As he stood next to what was to be his open grave, a passing colonel commanded the squad to stop and ordered Ouspensky to work for the White Army instead. Much later in his life he said he was too shocked by this experience to be afraid, but he looked down at the grass and "thought that he had never seen such extraordinary beauty."[193] He also witnessed an unarmed captive killed by sabers. For the rest of his life, Ouspensky abhorred the death of living creatures.

Ouspensky worked as a laborer at several dangerous jobs, including a coal mine, until he accepted a contract for working at a foundry in France in 1926. After a serious injury, he went to Paris to work in a bicycle factory. In 1929 Ouspensky entered a new Academy of Arts in Paris and eventually stopped working at the factory. This first formation of an academy did not last long, but during his time there Ouspensky met his first wife, as well as Gregory Kroug.[194] His first marriage was short, and he married his second wife, Lydia, in 1942.[195]

During this time Ouspensky painted his first icon, but he did so due to a dare from a friend who said it was very difficult. He painted the icon and then destroyed it, "realizing he had done something inappropriate."[196] However, through his interest in the icon he returned to Orthodoxy. Along with Kroug, he joined a group of theologians, artists, and intellectuals called the Stavropegial Brotherhood of St. Photios, and through the brotherhood he met the theologian Vladimir Lossky. The brotherhood took a leadership role in the Orthodox Church in Paris, clarifying Orthodoxy and witnessing to the centrality of the Eucharist and the liturgy.[197]

---

192. Doolan, *Rediscovering the Icon*, 11.
193. Ibid., 12.
194. Ibid.
195. Ibid.
196. Ibid.
197. Ibid.

The brotherhood's work of evangelization was cut short by the German occupation of Paris during World War II. Ouspensky went underground to avoid working in the German military plants and devoted himself to sacred painting, wood carving, and icon restoration since he could not work for secular patrons. After the war the brotherhood established the Institut St. Denis, and Vladimir Lossky served as the rector. Ouspensky began teaching a course in icon painting and continued to teach the course for forty years. In 1952 he wrote *The Meaning of Icons* with Lossky, and it became one of the primary works that brought the theology of the icon to contemporary readers. Ouspensky's other significant book, the two-volume *Theology of the Icon*, was first published in 1960; a revised edition was published in 1980. He also wrote many articles in response to questions about a variety of subjects within iconography.[198]

Ouspensky worked up to fourteen hours a day, moving among icon painting, carving, and restoration. He would write in the evenings, during which he "wrote with difficulty, slowly, and with great effort. He said, before his death, that he had not yet managed to say what was, in his view, the most important thing."[199] Leonid and Lydia Ouspensky had their Soviet citizenship restored in 1946, and they were able to return to Russia several times, which allowed Ouspensky to conduct research and study the ancient icons firsthand. Ouspensky died on December 12, 1987, and is buried in the Russian cemetery of Sainte-Geneviéve-des-Bois.[200]

We may draw several insights from this brief description of the icon in twentieth-century Russia and the life of Ouspensky that can be incorporated into the study of iconography. First is the resistance, sometimes referred to as spiritual warfare, which occurs as the work moves forward and as iconographers are drawn to this vocation. When the Spirit is moving toward unity and peace, virtues that come through the icon, we will encounter forces of disillusion, division, and chaos. This should be expected so that those who are moving further into the work of the icon are not unnecessarily frightened by this but learn to address it through prayer and the guidance of his or her spiritual elders.

Second, we have the role of the community, the community of iconographers, of all those who serve the church through the liturgical arts, and of the church as a whole. In Ouspensky's biography, we see this

198. Ibid., 14.
199. Ibid.
200. Ibid.

unfolding through his part in the Institut St. Denis and his life with the parish of Sainte-Geneviéve-des-Bois. Each iconographer needs to be integrated into the faith life of their own home community, whether it is a parish or a religious community. This is in addition to, of course, the Christian life of the home that the laity have with their spouses, children, other family members, or friends.

Third, we have the responsibility as iconographers to share the tradition with others. This is a joy, not a burden. We take up the work, sacrifices, and the martyrdom of our predecessors with gratitude and humility. At the appropriate time, a trained iconographer may accept his or her own students, becoming established on the other side of the master and apprentice relationship. Additionally, because so many non-Orthodox iconographers find themselves in settings where the understanding of the icon is limited, they also have many opportunities to educate their families, friends, and coworkers in a variety of settings. Any moment in which they introduce others to the presence of an icon, beautiful and still, is an opening for God's grace.

3

Inviting Others into the Conversation

Application

> *In icons the contradictions of this world are resolved: here, God is "all in all."*
>
> —Irina Yazykova

During the course of working on this book, the possibilities that I have to share iconography with others have increased in number and variety. These developments are a wonderful opportunity to shape what I have learned to suit the needs of people in a variety of settings. While my primary audience has been the Catholic seminarians at Mount Angel Seminary, the materials I have developed are suitable for other settings as well. Therefore I have included below materials for some of those settings. Finally, I will conclude with a discussion of possible future projects. My hope here is to serve as an example for other students and teachers of the icon and ecumenism who wish to bring their study of these subjects to the people they serve as well.

The Iconographic Arts Institute

Since my own introduction to iconography has come through the Iconographic Arts Institute, I will begin with a further explanation of the institute itself and an example of a presentation suitable to both the institute and seminarians. Thus far in the West, there are not any full-time programs in which a person may train as an iconographer, either through apprenticeships or a program that uses a larger group. The most common format of instruction in iconography in the United States at this time is a five- to seven-day workshop in which the students focus on completing a particular image that has been determined beforehand by the instructors. The Iconographic Arts Institute in Oregon fits this category with its seven-day summer institute. While full-time training is ideal, those in the West with a calling to iconography can take advantage of the opportunities that are currently available and work as well as they are able under their current circumstances so as to receive and develop the iconographic tradition in the West. Perhaps in this situation, we can apply one of the principles of receptive ecumenism, that our learning about other Christians need not be directly dependent on their willingness or even availability to instruct us, even if those circumstances are more the ideal. When this principle is applied to those called to iconography in the West, we have more hope. If we take responsibility for our own learning, reception and development of the tradition may still occur, even when full-time programs or other more extensive and direct instruction are not readily available.

As mentioned above, the Iconographic Arts Institute is the most extensive program most readily available in my area. Each year the institute welcomes between twenty-five and thirty students who range from beginners with little or no experience with art or the icon to advanced or practicing students who accept commissions and may teach their own students as well. Many of the advanced students have been attending the institute for more than ten years. Students primarily come from the western United States; some come from other areas of the United States, as well as Canada and Taiwan. The students range in age from their teens to their eighties and come from a variety of occupations and areas of expertise, particularly education, ministry, and medicine. Many of the students are Roman Catholic, and a variety of Protestant denominations are also represented. A few Orthodox Christians have attended the institute.

I was first introduced to the institute when it started holding its summer session at Queen of Angels Monastery in Mount Angel, Oregon, in 2004. Between 2004 and 2008, I offered some presentations on the Rule of Saint Benedict to the students of the institute, particularly on chapter 57, "The Artisans of the Monastery." I first attended the institute as a beginning student in 2009, and in 2010 I started individual lessons with Mary

Katsilometes, one of the institute instructors. At present, I have continued lessons with another institute instructor, Kathy Sievers. I continued to attend the institute as an intermediate student from 2010 through 2012. While working on my doctor of ministry and its dissertation project in 2013 and 2014, I took part in the institute in a new way rather than starting a new icon by working as a studio assistant during the week, helping the instructors with logistics and demonstrations and doing photography for the institute as well.

The Iconographic Arts Institute began as an artists' retreat at Mount Angel Abbey, the men's Benedictine community in St. Benedict, Oregon, and about a mile from the Benedictine Sisters of Mount Angel at Queen of Angels Monastery. One of the sessions of the retreat focused on iconography. In 1987, this retreat became the Iconography Institute, with Charles Rohrbacher of Juneau, Alaska, as the instructor. Kathy Sievers joined as an instructor in 1994, and Mary Katsilometes joined as an instructor in 1997. Between 1992 and 1998, Kathy Sievers and Mary Katsilometes studied in France with Father Egon Sendler, SJ, author of *Icon: Image of the Invisible*. The institute started teaching a beginner's session in 1997, and sessions of the institute were held at the Franciscan Renewal Center in Portland, Oregon, and at Mount Angel Abbey. In 2000 Charles Rohrbacher resigned from the institute and Claudia Coose joined the teaching staff.[1]

The next few years brought several new developments and opportunities. Mary Katsilometes and Kathy Sievers designed a structured curriculum that moves students from a simple icon of the Holy Face through complex icons with multiple figures and architecture. In 2005 the Iconography Institute was renamed the Iconographic Arts Institute when it became a nonprofit organization. In the summer of 2005, two institute instructors and ten students toured major icon sites in Russia, and during the academic year of 2006–2007, the institute instructors taught Byzantine drawing courses in Portland.[2]

In 2007, a teaching assistant, Ania Kouerek-Williams, joined the staff and started working with the beginning students, and she has had full responsibility for the beginning students since 2014. Also in 2007, the institute offered its first practicum experience for advanced students. In 2007 the students wrote a triptych of the Holy Face with Two Angels for St. Agatha Parish in Portland, and in 2009 the instructors and students

1. Sievers, "History of the Iconographic Arts Institute."
2. Ibid.

completed another triptych of the Protecting Veil of the Mother of God for the chapel of Queen of Angels Monastery. For several years starting in 2008, the institute also offered an illuminated manuscript course taught by Jean Germano.[3] From 2010 to 2013 the curriculum for the intermediate and advanced students focused on the four evangelists.

The Holy Face

3. Ibid.

Institute instructor Kathy Sievers has developed a list of ten characteristics that distinguish the Iconographic Arts Institute from other programs that are currently offered in many places in the West. These characteristics shape each part of the institute and encourage each student to find his or her place in relationship to the icon. They also serve as the basis for the Certificate in the Iconographic Arts, which the institute began offering in 2016. Each step of the curriculum requires an icon of appropriate difficulty, theological reading that supports the making of the icon for each step, and an essay, presentation, or other material that provides an avenue for the students to share their learning with others.

The first characteristic, introduction as inquiry, indicates that the whole institute is offered as an experience of adult Christian formation that starts with a period of inquiry, and through discernment, moves into formation, commitment, and service. In the beginner's class, students are invited into the vocation of an iconographer through learning about the canon of iconography and the life of prayer in which the writing of an icon is grounded. Characteristic number two is the twelve-step curriculum developed by Mary Katsilometes and Kathy Sievers. Beginners start with the Holy Face, and then move to a frontal bust, followed by a frontal standing figure. More complicated icons follow: multiple frontal figures, three-quarters turned figures, then multiple figures, architecture, and landscape.[4] This structured curriculum frees the student from leaping too far ahead into projects beyond their current skills, thus reducing their frustration and discouragement.

Spirituality, the third characteristic, mirrors the curriculum. Students are introduced to a grounded spiritual practice that builds on their current spirituality and sometimes introduces them to new ways of prayer. They are encouraged to seek spiritual direction, both during the institute and throughout the year. The first morning of the institute, the students receive a blessing of their hands, and the last morning the students and their completed work are blessed before they return home. Each day's work in the studio also begins with the iconographer's prayer and the blessing of each student by the instructors. Communion with and veneration of the saints is encouraged through the presence of many icons in the studio. Overall, as instructor Kathy Sievers explains, "The studio set up, daily prayer in the studio . . . and learning the language of iconography—all combine in

---

4. Sievers, "Ten Elements of the Iconographic Arts Institute."

the spiritual discipline of iconography."[5] As these practices come together, students may begin to experience the spirituality of the iconographer as a spirituality that infuses their whole life.

The next four characteristics flesh out different elements of the institute's curriculum. The institute provides theological instruction appropriate to each icon, instruction that includes consideration of the origins of the icon and the place of the icon in the world today. Guest speakers at the institute have included priests, religious and laypeople with expertise in Christology, Scripture, patristics, historical theology, and Christian spirituality. The experience of many religious communities has also been represented by the speakers, including Benedictines, Franciscans, Holy Names, Jesuits, and Missionaries of the Holy Spirit.[6]

As they learn about the theology of their particular icons, the students also learn about the geometry, aesthetic elements, and color theory of icons. With the geometry, the students "are introduced to revelation of the design of the icon that has been handed down through generations."[7] The students analyze the geometry in their icons and learn how the balance and harmony of an icon are the result of its geometric structure. Through the geometry the students learn proportion as well, which enables them to make an icon of any size. As they study the icon's aesthetic elements, the students learn the fundamentals of figure drawing, including the characteristics of Byzantine figures. They also learn about inverse perspective as they draw architecture and landscapes. For color theory, beginning students work with color wheels and mixing the most common colors in iconography, and advanced students study more complex color. For painting their icons, students learn to use egg tempera, the traditional medium for icons.[8]

Instruction with the above seven elements leads directly to the eighth element: empowerment of the institute participants. By the end of their week at the institute, students have enough basic skills to work and practice on their own. While at the institute, the students are encouraged to try a variety of techniques and exercises, all of which are opportunities to learn more. During the institute and as they return home, the students are also introduced to the ninth element, the ministry of service. Beginning students learn that their icon panels were made by last year's

5. Ibid.
6. Ibid.
7. Ibid.
8. Ibid.

beginning students, and the true gesso panels they make will be used by next year's beginners. Advanced students may work with other students through the practicum.[9]

The last element frames all of the rest of the elements and the whole experience of the institute. When Kathy Sievers and Mary Katsilometes studied in France with Fr. Egon Sendler, he explained to his students from around the world that as they studied the icon, they would create the icon of community. As the US affiliate of Fr. Sendler's community, the Iconographic Arts Institute also places great value on the relationships formed through their work. "Lasting friendships are created," explains Kathy Sievers, and "the challenging work of portraying the Incarnate Christ, and the dramatic finish of the institute, steeped in prayer, bond the participants."[10] I can personally attest to the generosity, kindness, and friendship offered to me by my fellow students at the institute. The time with them is precious, and the bond remains throughout the year as we pursue the icon in our home communities.

---

9. Ibid.
10. Ibid.

The Mother of God

Given the richness of the above ten elements, the presentation below is just one example of the talks and materials that I may offer as a supplement to the curriculum of the Iconographic Arts Institute. The possibilities will naturally shift depending on which icons are the focus of the curriculum each year. I would also like to draw on more materials from the rich tradition of Orthodox theology since the students attending the institute, even if they have had some theological education, may not have been exposed to this part of the Christian theological tradition.

The elements for a presentation below on an icon of the Last Judgment draw on materials from my course in theological anthropology at Mount Angel Seminary with Dr. Katy Leamy. We are not as familiar with this icon in the West, and its imagery may seem strange at first. Within the current format of the institute, a presentation such as this is usually about an hour, including time for questions and discussion, and may occur either in the evening after dinner or in the morning after the opening prayer and blessing. The institute instructors have also been experimenting with shorter presentations throughout the day. Regardless of when it occurs, presenters for the institute need to take into account that the students not only come from various places within the Christian tradition, but they also may be quite tired depending on when during the week the presentation occurs. At times it may be more productive to offer the students some shorter materials or presentations.

Since the material below is just some elements for a handout rather than the entire presentation, I will offer a few explanatory points here. Judgment, particularly in our individualistic society and regardless of whether it originates from another person or from God, is not an acceptable stance to many people. The verse from 1 Corinthians at the top of the handout reminds everyone that ultimately judgment is about love, about being fully known by God so that we may fully love him. The chord structure of eschatology, which I have drawn from Dr. Leamy's lectures, explains that the fundamental features of human life will be both maintained and radically transformed after our death. The next section offers material on the Last Judgment from a variety of Christian sources, in particular the Russian Orthodox theologian Sergius Bulgakov. A portion of his book *The Bride of the Lamb* was the focus of my major project for Theological Anthropology. His material gives a key definition of eternal life. Eternal life is not endless time; rather, it is the pervasive presence of God in which the Last Judgment occurs. The final passage from Bulgakov is the most important: each of our lives contains virtue and sin, and God will certainly handle this complexity far better than we do. The rest of the handout explains features of the icon of the Last Judgment. The example I've drawn on for this explanation is from the Museum of Russian Icons in Massachusetts; ideally I would also bring other examples to illustrate the other possible variations on this icon.

Our Experience of the Last or Eternal Judgment: A Short Presentation for the Iconographic Arts Institute

1. "For now we see in a mirror, dimly, but then we will see face to face. Now I know only in part; then I will know fully, even as I have been fully known. And now faith, hope, and love abide, these three; and the greatest of these is love" (1 Cor 13:12–13).

2. The Chord Structure of Eschatology: "Human origins and human freedom, the physical and spiritual nature of human life, our experience of history, time, progress, and culture, the variety of human experience of fear, love, joy, and grief, and our human failures of sin, corruption, injustice, and suffering: after death all of these have continuity and radical difference."

3. The *Catechism of the Catholic Church*, par. 1039: "In the presence of Christ, who is Truth itself, the truth of each man's relationship with God will be laid bare. The Last Judgment will reveal even to the furthest consequences the good each person has done or failed to do during his earthly life."

4. Robert Jenson passage #1: "In Scripture, judgment is intervention to restore righteousness, that is, to set a community right. . . . The *Last Judgment* is simply a judgment that encompasses the entire human community and after which another will not be needed" (38).

5. Robert Jenson passage #2: "This setting right should not be seen as a sort of preliminary, clearing the decks for the establishment of universal bliss. This setting right is itself the *content* of the eternal event of bliss. What happens as final salvation? Precisely that *we are set right* with each other, that I have the joy of God's rebuke for my sin against my brothers and sisters, and the joy of seeing the repair of my injuries to them, at my cost. The point is of fundamental importance, for it is just so that it is me, in my identity as the sinner I am, who lives in the joy of the kingdom. The blessed eternity will be as it were the eternal expansion of one great reconciling" (39).

6. Sergius Bulgakov passage #1: "Thus, eternal life, or eternity, is a special quality of the life of the future age, which will pass not apart from and in isolation from God, as our age does, but in His knowledge, as life in God" (469).

7. Sergius Bulgakov passage #2: "The creaturely nature of human beings with its freedom is not annihilated even when it encounters God's eternity and is thereby immersed in eternal life, in the light of God's face. This encounter . . . corresponds to what Scripture calls judgment and verdict: a human being sees himself in the justice of eternity, in his supra-eternal aspect as God conceived him (this is the measure of the talents given to him). All self-evaluations are accomplished by him in the light of this eternity" (473).

8. Sergius Bulgakov passage #3: "The mystery here, which, as usual, bears the stamp of an antinomy, is that the very distinction between heaven and hell exists only for our limited earthly condition. But since every human being sins, the two states inevitably coexist in one and the same person. One state does not abolish the other, but one or the other is dominant. Hidden from us are God's judgments, which can compensate or even abolish our sins in the definitive verdict, according to His mercy. But the opposite question can also be asked: Are good works that precede the fall also annulled, or is their existence a supplementary burden? Does Judas the Apostle intercede with his apostolic ministry for Judas the Betrayer? Does the apostle Peter, who, contrary to his apostleship, renounced Christ, bear the torments of punishment for this renunciation? *The mixture of good and evil that is proper to the overwhelming majority of human beings compels us to postulate not a simple but a complex sum total of God's judgment, which unites blessing and condemnation. This mystery of life of the future age surpasses our understanding*" (475).

Some Details of the Icon of the Last Judgment: Universal Resurrection

1. The Small Deesis: Christ is in the middle, with the Mother of God and John the Baptist on either side of him. Their prayers indicate a plea for salvation that continues until the last day.

2. The Apostles: Includes Paul and Luke; they hold open books with phrases drawn from the Orthodox liturgy, prayers, and oral folklore traditions. An example: "I know, My God, that your judgment is necessary for all people. Confess."

3. The Heavenly Jerusalem: Saints seated at a table set for a feast and celebrating the victory over evil; figures include prophets, bishops, tsars, warriors, and virtuous wives. An inscription in the margins of the icon reads: "All saints will start rejoicing and celebrate the birth of Christ along with the saintly angels."

4. The Hand of God and the Serpent of Tribulations: A naked youth: only the good deeds performed during his lifetime will protect him from the serpent. Each circle of the serpent represents a tribulation or measurement of sin through which each soul must pass. Sins are listed in order of gravity: lying, greed, denunciation, idle chatter, anger, blasphemy, gluttony, drunkenness, slander, foul language, adultery, fornication, unjust condemnation to jail, vanity, striving for excess wealth, self-love, despair, murder, self-glorification, and pride.

5. The Kindly Adulterer: a naked man tied to a pillar of shame and located exactly in the central axis. Scroll with his penalty: "For the sake of alms you are relieved of torments, but because of fornication are deprived as well of paradise." Seems to depict a folk tradition that is in tension with the official Orthodox position that does not recognize an interim state between heaven and hell.

Bibliography

1. Bulgakov, Sergius. "The Eternal in the Temporal (On the Eternity of Bliss and Torments)." In *The Bride of the Lamb*, 466–519. Grand Rapids: Eerdmans, 2002.

2. Cleenewerck, Laurent A. *His Broken Body: Understanding and Healing the Schism between the Roman Catholic and Eastern Orthodox Churches*. Washington, DC: Euclid University Consortium Press, 2007.

3. Jenson, Robert W. "The Great Transformation." In *The Last Things: Biblical and Theological Perspectives on Eschatology*, edited by Carl E. Braaten and Robert W. Jenson, 33–42. Grand Rapids: Eerdmans, 2002.

4. Knorre, Boris K. "Icon of the Last Judgment: A Detailed Analysis." *The Museum of Russian Icons*. http://www.museumofrussianicons.org/wp-content/uploads/2016/09/KnorreLastJudgmentFinal.pdf.

INVITING OTHERS INTO THE CONVERSATION

Mount Angel Seminary

My responsibilities at Mount Angel Seminary have provided many opportunities for teaching about the icon and incorporating the icon into different classes and assignments. In addition to the classroom, I have the opportunity for individual conversations with those who visit my office, both students and colleagues, and to share with them the icons, prayer cards, and other materials I have gathered there to support these conversations. Several colleagues have also invited me to give presentations in their courses, including Humanities II, a college-level course that focuses on the Middle Ages, and a graduate-level Scripture course on the Prophets. My presentation for Prophets focused on an explanation of the icon of the Mother of God of the Sign, an icon that is intimately connected to the prophet Isaiah. I developed slideshows for these presentations, and I have also offered presentations that were open to the wider seminary community using these materials.

I have also made slideshows from the photographs I have taken during several sessions of the Iconographic Arts Institute, and they are proving to be one of my best tools for explaining the work and spirit of the institute. Usually I silently run the slideshow, which lasts about twenty minutes, thus making time for the icons to speak for themselves. I then answer questions, drawing on the knowledge I have gained from my experience as a student of the institute and the materials in the first two sections of this book.

Writing in the Humanities

For five years one of my teaching responsibilities at Mount Angel Seminary was a course entitled Writing in the Humanities; this is the seminary's version of freshman composition. The course focuses on writing relatively short essays with a clear and well-supported thesis statement. The readings and essay assignments may be drawn from a variety of subject areas within the humanities, including poetry and fiction, religious studies, rhetoric and composition, and the arts. Thus, I have worked to select readings and design essay assignments that will stretch my students' interests in religious subjects and challenge them to improve their writing and communication with their intended audience.

For Writing in the Humanities, I have developed a series of assignments and activities that focus on a large mosaic of the Annunciation in the lobby of one of the main buildings of Mount Angel Seminary. The first activity introduces the students to the meaning of color in iconography. I give each student line drawings of several icons and a new box of sixteen crayons. Of course many of them have not had a new box of crayons since they were children, so that is part of the fun! As I share a verbal explanation of the meaning of each color, the students fill in the appropriate areas in their drawings. They also receive a handout about color that draws from *Hidden and Triumphant: The Underground Struggle to Save Russian Iconography*, by Irina Yazykova. The information they learn in this activity builds into a writing assignment, an in-class essay in which they write a detailed description of the color, composition, and subject of the mosaic of the Annunciation. Then, building on the information they gather from the in-class essay, the students write an outside essay in which they develop a theme of their own choosing that they draw from the mosaic.

In-Class Essay #1: Describing an Image

In your essay, write a detailed description of the mosaic of the Annunciation in the lobby of Annunciation Hall. Use your description to demonstrate you have carefully and thoroughly observed the mosaic. The introductory paragraph and thesis statement should give the reader a hint of the description you will offer in the rest of your essay. Your description should focus on three areas: composition, color, and identification. Composition should address the arrangement of the figures and other elements in the mosaic, and color should address the placement and use of color throughout the mosaic. The section on identification should explain how the viewer might know who the figures are in the mosaic. You may paraphrase but not directly quote the Gospel of Luke. You may also wish to discuss the location and placement of the mosaic in this section. Focus on your description as a neutral reporter; do not include your own opinion or analysis in your essay.

Outside Essay #2: Analyzing an Image

Write a three- to four-page essay in which you explain your main response to the Annunciation mosaic. Your thesis statement should be clearly stated and a more elegant version of "My main response to the Annunciation mosaic is _____." Your essay should include a substantial amount of the material from your description of the mosaic. Your reader should be able to understand how your response is built on your discussion of the composition, color, and identification of the mosaic. Your analysis may focus on a particular theme, a memory evoked by the mosaic, or questions that arose as you considered the mosaic. What surprised you? What perplexed you? What questions do you still have that you would like to explore further? Give your essay an appropriate title, and make sure it is in the proper MLA format.

History of Art

During my time teaching at Mount Angel Seminary, I was offered another opportunity that takes advantage of the experience I have gained with iconography. Mount Angel Seminary offers a course entitled History of Art, a required course for College Four seminarians, a portion of which I dedicated to iconography. In the iconography portion, I included historical and theological background as well as some hands-on experience with the materials and techniques of iconography. The elements of the course I include below explain the major assignments and activities for the course. The combination of the two portions of the course found in the course description has helped me to put the icon in a larger historical context for my own studies and for my students. Since students in the setting of the seminary were often curious about icons, I encouraged them to choose an icon for one of their two observation essays and to consider including icons in the materials they chose to illustrate the theme they selected for their museum exhibits.

Saint Matthew

Course Elements:

1. Course Description: The first and larger portion of this course is a survey of the history of art and architecture in the Western world from Greco-Roman origins to the present. The second and smaller portion is an introduction to the theology, aesthetics, and technique of iconography. In addition to introducing the student to the fundamentals of art, architecture, and iconography, the course will offer

opportunities to develop and reflect on our responses to art, both verbally and in writing.

2. Texts and Materials: *Art across Time*, 4th edition, by Laurie Schneider Adams; *Icons and Saints of the Eastern Orthodox Church*, by Alfredo Tradigo and Stephen Sartarelli; additional class handouts and art supplies provided in class.

3. Art Exercises: During the portion of our course dedicated to iconography, you will complete several exercises, both in and out of class. Your exercises are assessed according to the quality of your effort, not your artistic ability. I will announce in class when particular exercises will be due.

4. Observation Essays: Select two works of art to be the focus of two separate essays. One work must be pre-1800 and one work must be post-1800. In each essay, write a detailed description of your work of art that demonstrates you have observed your work of art as carefully and thoroughly as possible. Your description should include information about the subject, composition, and color of your work of art. Your introduction should also include some brief background information about its creation and historical context. Each essay must be a minimum of two pages and include an appropriate two-part title. Also attach a good color copy your work of art to each essay. Each essay must be in the MLA format and be free of typographical and grammatical errors.

5. Museum Exhibit and Presentation: For your exhibit, select ten to fifteen works and organize them around a theme of your choosing. The theme may not be a particular time period or focus on the work of just one artist. Your slides must include a reproduction of each work accompanied by its title, artist, date, dimensions, and media. Your slides must also include a clear title and acknowledgments. Include portions of your curator's statement in your slides as well. Your curator's statement must be a minimum of two pages, include an appropriate two-part title, and include a bibliography of the sources of the materials used in your exhibit. In your statement, explain the significance of your theme and its importance to the community of Mount Angel Seminary. Your statement must be in the MLA format, and both your exhibit and your statement must be free of typographical and grammatical errors.

Theology of Art

During my time at Mount Angel Seminary, I developed an elective on a theology of art, which I taught for two semesters and, as with History of Art, included iconography as a significant element of the course. The course as a whole is based on two principles. First, given the possible breadth of a course entitled Theology of Art, I chose to focus on visual art, including but not limited to iconography. Second, I chose a methodology that is more of an intuitive rather than systematic approach to the subject. Rather than structured lectures, our class meetings alternated between class discussions and sketchbook exercises. The discussions were based on handouts I wrote that draw together passages from Scripture, Church documents, and other sources that may be used to develop a theology of art. These passages and their discussion provide part of the basis for the theological reflections, which are explained below. The sketchbook exercises offer the students the opportunity to learn some of the techniques, particularly drawing, that support the making of an icon and in at least a small way the opportunity to be creators of beauty themselves, a point that is key to David Clayton's *The Way of Beauty*, which serves as the text for the course. Each sketchbook exercise includes the materials needed for the exercise, the components of the exercise done inside and outside of class, and some additional Scripture or other materials that further support or illustrate a given exercise. The day dedicated to the third exercise, included below, also includes discussion and examples of the features of Byzantine faces in traditional iconography.

The Pantocrator

Course Elements:

1. Course Description: Theology of Art focuses on the scriptural and theological basis for our experience and creation of art, particularly the visual arts, in both secular and sacred contexts. As part of their study, students will take part in hands-on experience with making icons and other visual art.

2. Texts and Materials: *The Way of Beauty*, by David Clayton; art supply kit purchased through the seminary bookstore; a Bible with which you already study and pray; a copy of the documents of the Second Vatican Council; additional readings and handouts given in class.

3. Sketchbook: On the second class day of each week, our work will focus on exercises and activities that are part of creating an icon or other visual art. Your exercises will be assessed according to the quality of your effort, not your artistic ability. Your sketchbook work will also include contributing to our common collage materials. Your sketchbooks will be due the last week of class. By the end of the semester, you should have at least one version of each exercise in your sketchbooks. In addition to these, your sketchbook should include at least fifteen more versions of exercises of your choosing. For instance, you may repeat one exercise fifteen more times, or you may repeat three exercises five more times.

4. Theological Reflection: Theological reflection is a process of bringing the theological tradition, in our case elements of a theology of art, to bear on our lived experience. The thesis or main idea for your reflection should be at least one insight you have received by this point in the course. While I am not looking for a specific length for your reflection, a well-done reflection should take at least three pages to sufficiently explore and support your main insight. Your theological reflection should include: (1) The story of your encounter with an art-related experience this semester in which you were a participant or a viewer. Your story may include your work with any of our sketchbook exercises this semester. (2) The impact of this encounter: Why was this encounter significant to you? (3) How does this experience relate to the readings on a theology of art that we have discussed in class? (4) Discussion of what new insight this encounter offers you about the place of art in our experience of God and of the church. (5) Discussion of how you may bring this new insight to your current work and studies, as well as your future ministry. Your reflection must also be in the MLA format, have a suitable two-part title, and be free of grammatical and typographical errors.

5. *The Way of Beauty* Book Review: For this essay, you will write a book review of *The Way of Beauty*, by David Clayton. In a book review, you are offering the reader a glimpse into the content of a book, as well as

a description of your experience reading the book. Your review should be three to five pages and contain the following elements: (1) A summary of the content of the book, including the main thesis around which it is organized. Your summary should include points from each chapter of the book. (2) A description of your experience reading the book. What ideas did you have about this subject before reading this book? How did those ideas change through reading this book? What surprised you? How has this book contributed to your experience of our class on a theology of art? (3) Some background about the author that goes beyond the description found in the book. Where does the author currently work? What are some of his publications or other experiences that qualify him to write *The Way of Beauty*? (4) Examine the books and other materials found in the footnotes. Which books or other materials are available in the Mount Angel Abbey Library? Which one or two books from the footnotes draw you the most? (5) Outside of the students in Theology of Art, to whom would you recommend this book? For instance, which other classes might find it useful? In a parish setting, which staff, volunteers, or parishioners might find it the most useful or interesting? (6) A two-part title (a title and subtitle), as well as the proper MLA format.

Sketchbook Exercise #3: Drawing Facial Features and Hands and Feet

1. Materials: sketchbook, drawing pencil set, T-square, sample drawings of eyes, noses, and mouths, and prototypes of the Holy Face, other icons, and the hands and feet in an icon.
2. Work in class: Complete a set of ten facial features—eyes, noses, or mouths—and complete a set of five hands and feet.
3. For your sketchbook outside of class: Complete a second set of ten facial features—eyes, noses, or mouths—and complete a second set of five hands and feet.
4. Mark 10:21: And Jesus, looking upon him loved him, and said to him, "You are lacking one thing; go, sell what you have, and give to the poor, and you will have treasure in heaven; and come, follow me."

5. *In addition to the above passage from Mark, this handout also includes two prayers, "Christ Has No Body," from Saint Teresa of Avila, and "We Awaken in Christ's Body," from Saint Symeon the New Theologian.*

Sketchbook Exercise #5: Drawing and Applying Gold Assist

1. Materials: sketchbook, drawing pencils, erasers, gold leaf, size, brushes, and icon prototypes.

2. Work in class: draw two stars from the garments of the Mother of God or two other sections of gold assist and practice applying gold assist.

3. For your sketchbook outside of class: draw five more stars or sections of gold assist.

4. Exodus 34:29–30: When Moses came down from Mount Sinai, with the two tables of the testimony in his hand as he came down from the mountain, Moses did not know that the skin of his face shone because he had been talking with God. And when Aaron and all the people of Israel saw Moses, behold, the skin of his face shone, and they were afraid to come near him.

5. Revelation 21:23–24: And the city has no need of sun or moon to shine upon it, for the glory of God is its light, and its lamp is the Lamb. By its light shall the nations walk; and the kings of the earth shall bring their glory to it, and its gates shall never be shut by day—and there shall be no night there; they shall bring into it the glory and the honor of the nations.

Sketchbook Exercise #6: Initials and Lettering

1. Materials: sketchbook, drawing pencils, erasers, T-square or other straight edge, prototypes, and graph paper.

2. Work in class: complete on your graph paper three names or sets of initials.

3. For your sketchbook outside of class: complete three more names or sets of initials.

4. John 20:31: But these are written that you may believe that Jesus is the Christ, the Son of God, and believing you may have life in his name.

5. Philippians 2:9–11: Therefore God has highly exalted him and bestowed on him the name which is above every name, that at the name of Jesus every knee should bow, in heaven and on earth and under the earth, and every tongue confess that Jesus Christ is Lord, to the glory of God the Father.

6. Revelation 22:1–5: Then he showed me the river of the water of life, bright as crystal, flowing from the throne of God and of the Lamb through the middle of the street of the city; also, on either side of the river, the tree of life with its twelve kinds of fruit, yielding its fruit each month; and the leaves of the tree were for the healing of the nations. There shall no more be anything accursed, but the throne of God and of the Lamb shall be in it, and his servants shall worship him; they shall see his face, and his name shall be on their foreheads. And night shall be no more; they need no light of lamp or sun, for the Lord will be their light, and they shall reign for ever and ever.

Additional Seminary Talks

In addition to the materials I have developed for specific classes, I have also developed materials for groups at the seminary outside of the classroom, two examples of which I am including here. The first example is two short talks given to a student-led and organized study group that focused on ecumenism, particularly in relation to the Orthodox. This group actively engaged in the receptive ecumenism I discussed above. In the first talk, I discussed examples from within our own archdiocese that illustrate how the iconographic tradition has been integrated into several Catholic churches in ways that respect both the elements of the iconographic tradition as discussed above and the ways the Catholic liturgical tradition differs from the Orthodox liturgical tradition. Before discussing these examples, I explain the layout of an Orthodox iconostasis, as well as the general layout of iconography within an Orthodox church. I explain that due in part to their differing architecture, we cannot simply place the Orthodox scheme within a Catholic setting; we must study both the tradition and the new setting to find ways to integrate iconography that are appropriate and prayerful.

I use three icons as my examples: the icon of the Protecting Veil of the Mother of God in the chapel of Queen of Angels Monastery, the home of the Benedictine Sisters of Mount Angel; the icons of Saint Francis and Saint Clare at Saint Clare Catholic Church in Portland, Oregon; and the seven large icons at Resurrection Catholic Church in Tualatin, Oregon. The icon of the Protecting Veil, made through the hands of Mary Katsilometes, is a large triptych with the Mother of God in the middle with the Archangels Gabriel and Michael on either side of her and is an example of bringing an image that is common in the East to an appropriate setting in the West. Given that the monastery is dedicated to Mary, Queen of the Angels, this image is fitting as it represents the intercession and protection that the Mother of God has extended and continues to extend over the community and all those who visit the sisters' chapel. The icon also includes architecture that is easily recognizable as the home of the community, with the monastery and its giant sequoia tree behind Gabriel and the chapel with its distinctive lantern behind Michael. The icons of Saint Francis and Saint Clare, made through the hands of Kathy Sievers, also incorporate the local community into the icon on several levels. Part of the architecture is modeled on the architecture of the parish, and Kathy Sievers used some of the soil from the grounds of the parish to make the pigments she used to paint the icon.

My third example, seven large icons from Resurrection Catholic Church, is the most extensive example with which I have worked of incorporating the iconographic tradition into a Catholic setting. The icons are very large because they are incorporated into a building with a stark, modern design with very high ceilings. An icon of the Crucifixion is behind the altar; to the left of the altar is an icon of the Resurrection, and to the right of the altar is an icon of the Annunciation. Near the entrance to the church and the baptismal font is an icon of the Baptism, and on the opposite wall is an icon of Pentecost. At the time of this writing, several smaller icons are also being made by Mary Katsilometes and placed in niches along the wall to the right of the altar, near the reconciliation room, and in the adoration chapel. In the case of each icon, the layout of this modern Catholic church was taken into account as a traditional Orthodox image was put in an appropriate place. For instance, the icon of the Resurrection, which also honors the name of the parish, is not an image of the Resurrection of Christ but of his descent into Hades. He grasps the hands of Adam and Eve, pulling them out of their tombs, thus representing the salvation of all of humanity. I followed up this third example with a slide presentation composed of process photos I took while participating in the work of making the icons at Resurrection. I was among the students of Mary Katsilometes who assisted with her work, taking part in tasks such as applying gesso to the boards, laying down gold leaf, assisting with the painting, and helping to apply the olipha, the final varnish for the icons. I was present primarily for the varnishing, so I was able to capture many pictures of the icons close up, which would be much more challenging once they were installed high up on the walls of the church. I use these slides to illustrate for the seminarians what the process for such a large-scale project looks and feels like, for the iconographer responsible for the work, for her students, and for members of the community. I include several photos of members of the parish helping with the work as well, thus illustrating that the work of the icon, both physically and spiritually, is the work of the entire parish. Through the sharing and discussion of all three of these examples, I offer the seminarians a way into considering how they might invite iconographers to shape their own churches once they are priests and pastors.

My second example is a talk given during one of Mount Angel Seminary's alumni days, which was part of the overall program of prayer, social events, and intellectual input that was offered to them. As with all of the above work with the seminarians, a certain amount of experience with theology was in place with the alumni, whether they were clergy or laymen and laywomen. This talk is an example of how the work of bringing the iconographic tradition to Catholic seminaries can reach beyond its current students, and the aim of the talk was to invite the gathered alumni to expand their experience of theology through consideration of the icon, as well as to take part, even if only for the day, in a portion of receptive ecumenism. First, I provided the alumni with a solid introduction to the institute, including an explanation of its curriculum and the other components as explained above. Then I discussed with the alumni reasons for integrating the study of iconography into our study of theology by drawing on my own experience and studies, as well as that of other students of the Iconographic Arts Institute.

First, I explained that as a writer and a teacher, I spend most of my time soaked in words, and the icon offers a different experience. The icon is quiet. As with most visual artistic culture, the icon offers its witness without words, without verbal argument, persuasion, or flourish. The icon forms us through its visual language, its visual witness to the communion of saints and kingdom of God. Some like to spend time in contemplative prayer with an icon; I find I pray with them as an integral part of my surroundings. Second, I explained that the icon is the visual language of the church. Just as the Scriptures give us the written language of the church, the icon gives us the visual language of the church that developed before the great divide between East and West. This visual language includes geometry, the meaning of color, the significance of light and gold leaf, and the traits and features that help us to identify particular figures. For instance, icons of Christ always have his Greek initials; the Mother of God always has three gold stars on her garment; and Peter always has a gray beard. These explanations of the visual language of the icon draw on the same materials I use for my seminary courses. Third, I explained that, for me, iconography has become one of the primary means through which I continue to pursue theology after finishing my own studies at Mount Angel Seminary. As alumni of the seminary, I explained, we all have experience with doing theology, primarily through reading and writing, speaking and preaching. These are beautiful and fruitful ways to further our understanding of the mystery of God and of ministering to his people. Working as an iconographer and teaching about the icon is also a way of doing theology, of furthering my understanding and the understanding of others of the mystery of God. Through the icon, I picked up further theological work as I picked up a paintbrush, and the tools of iconography became a way of doing theological research, work, and reflection.

After these initial reasons, I touched on spiritual ecumenism and receptive ecumenism, drawing on the material discussed above. The ecumenical movement works for the union of the Christian community, grounded in the prayer of Christ in the Gospel of John 17:20–23. Spiritual ecumenism asks us to pray for Christian unity and to take up opportunities to pray with Christians outside of our communions. Given that the iconographic tradition was developed and nurtured by the Church in the East, our prayer with icons may also take part in the prayer for greater union between the Orthodox Church and the Roman Catholic Church. The icon is also an opportunity for receptive ecumenism. While ecumenical work is always grounded in prayer and our own conversion, receptive ecumenism gives some additional weight to our work. An underlying assumption of receptive ecumenism is that we are always starting in the middle, in our inherited stances and understandings. While taking those seriously it is also open to new insights, as learning is given priority over teaching and we take responsibility for our own education about the faith of others.

INVITING OTHERS INTO THE CONVERSATION

The Iconographic Tradition beyond Catholic Seminaries

My final example, while drawing on the materials I have developed for a Catholic seminary, also reaches beyond it. This may be, though, an appropriate example with which to conclude. Our seminarians, by and large, are not being formed to remain in the seminary, though some may later return for a time as professors, formation directors, or spiritual directors. They are being formed to minister to the people in their parishes in all of their complexity and variety, as well as to serve as witnesses to those beyond the boundaries of the parish, Christian and non-Christian alike. Thus, I conclude here with a day-long class I recently offered through my local arts association. The group that attended, though only about a dozen people, included Catholics, other Christians, and those with little or no religious background, all of whom had little previous knowledge of or experience with the icon but were willing to devote a day to exploring the language and meaning of iconography.

Since I was meeting with people who had experience with other kinds of art but not with iconography, after an initial introduction to my experience with the Iconographic Arts Institute, I started the day by defining some terms. The terms "iconography" and "iconology" have their own meanings within the study of art and art history. However, I was ensuring that when I was speaking of iconography, they knew I meant the traditional canon of sacred images that has been preserved and passed down through the Christian tradition, first through the undivided church and then primarily though not exclusively through the Orthodox Church. Individual icons, I explained, are the sacred images representing Christ, the Mother of God, and the saints that are in keeping with the Orthodox canon.

Next we moved into the aesthetics of the icon. With seminarians or other Christian groups, I would usually start with the primary theological principles behind the icon. However, this was a group whose primary interest lies in the doing, the making of art. Thus, while overall the material I shared with the arts association is similar to the material I share with seminarians, I reshaped the order and emphasis of the presentation to complement their backgrounds and interests.

I started with discussing the importance of prototypes, of making the selection of an ancient prototype the first step in creating a new icon. Next we moved to geometry, starting with the proportions of the board and then moving to analysis of the figures and their arrangement on the panel. After geometry we discussed color and how its use in iconography is guided by the traditional canon that explains the theological meaning each color is understood to convey. Discussing color also included discussing the role of light, particularly as it is represented by the use of gold in iconography. Following color was the use of line in iconography, lines that are fluid but not curved, since iconography uses composite lines for items such as garments. Last, we focused on the characteristics of Byzantine faces since the faces are the most important feature of any icon. All of these points of aesthetics were illustrated with examples of my own work, both my completed icons and drawing and other exercises from my sketchbooks, some of which served as examples for the hands-on portion of the class later in the day.

Only after our discussion of aesthetics did we move on to prayer and the theology of the icon. We can think of the iconographer as the monk of artists since prayer is essential to the calling and work of the iconographer. Within the world of visual art and all the ways in which art is made and experienced, the icon is explicitly located within the Christian tradition and a life of prayer. Put another way, the icon is first, foremost, and always a prayer, a prayer that moves in multiple directions. The daily work of the iconographer may include the traditional iconographer's prayer; this prayer is also used to begin each day of the Iconographic Arts Institute. Iconographers are also integrated into the prayer life of the church. Students come to the institute from a variety of Christian backgrounds, so the prayer within the life of the church is going to vary according to their traditions. Within the Catholic, Orthodox, and other liturgical traditions, it will include celebration of the sacraments, especially the Eucharist. It may also include all or portions of the Liturgy of the Hours. The praying of the psalms at regular intervals throughout the day sanctifies time and all of our activities, including our artwork in all of its forms. Last, iconographers and other students of the icon also find spiritual direction, the sharing and reflection upon one's spiritual journey with a wise guide, helpful and even necessary. Work with spiritual direction assists us with discerning the place of the icon in our lives, of our place in the spectrum of activities that involve iconography, which includes but is not limited to praying with icons, making icons a part of one's prayer, making icons for family and friends, offering talks or retreats that incorporate iconography, accepting commissions, and teaching one's own students. Just as all the colors on the spectrum have a value and a place, so do each of these activities.

I framed the short discussion of the theology of the icon with the arts association by asking, what does the experience of the icon imply about how

God approaches us, and what does it imply about how we approach God and one another? I used points from Aidan Hart's book *Techniques of Icon and Wall Painting* to support our discussion of theology, in part because, while his points are clearly conveyed, the vast majority of his book is concrete techniques that would be of interest to this group of artists. His explanation also worked well because he brings his discussion of theology back to aesthetics and technique and how they are used to convey the theology of the icon. After a break we brought our own activities back to aesthetics and technique as I offered the group a variety of drawing exercises to choose from during the rest of our time, including simple tracings of a prototype, tinker-toy drawings that analyzed the figures in a prototype, practice with facial features, and shading exercises with a figure's garments.

Given the opportunities I have already experienced as I have developed materials for Catholic seminarians and groups beyond the seminary, the materials I may develop as I keep pursuing the connections among ecumenism and the iconographic tradition may continue to surprise me. I certainly hope so! At the time of this writing, I may be offered further opportunities to develop presentations on ecumenism for the Iconographic Arts Institute, whether it be through brief oral presentations, slide presentations, or various handouts. If these materials were offered early in the week, additional thoughtful quotations pertaining to ecumenism could be put on the students' tables during the rest of the week. Perhaps ecumenism could be used as an overall theme for the week of the institute. Given some of the prominent examples of the use of traditional iconography within the Catholic tradition, including but not limited to those discussed above, the writing of some supporting materials for these icons may be another possible future project, including but not limited to brochures, booklets, and online materials. Last, my recent experience with my local arts association demonstrated to me that curiosity about the icon extends beyond our seminaries and parishes, and I may find additional ways to offer the icon and its ecumenical work to a wider scope of people than I originally thought might be possible. Regardless of the place or materials used, my hope remains to introduce many more to the beauty and joy of the icon.

Bibliography

Bartholomew. "Address by His All-Holiness Ecumenical Patriarch Bartholomew to His Holiness Pope Francis of Rome." Vatican, March 20, 2013. http://www.byzcath.org/index.php/news-mainmenu-49/3529-address-by-his-all-holiness-ecumenical-patriarch-bartholomew-to-his-holiness-pope-francis-of-rome.
Bigham, Steven. "The Icon: Sign of Unity or Division?" Pt. 1. *Orthodox Arts Journal*, June 8, 2012. https://www.orthodoxartsjournal.org/the-icon-sign-of-unity-or-division/.
———. "The Icon: Sign of Unity or Division?" Pt. 2. *Orthodox Arts Journal*, June 15, 2012. https://www.orthodoxartsjournal.org/the-icon-sign-of-unity-or-division-pt-2/.
———. "The Icon: Sign of Unity or Division?" Pt. 3. *Orthodox Arts Journal*, June 22, 2012. https://www.orthodoxartsjournal.org/the-icon-sign-of-unity-or-division-some-other-points-pt-3/.
———. "The Icon: Sign of Unity or Division?" Pt. 4. *Orthodox Arts Journal*, June 29, 2012. https://www.orthodoxartsjournal.org/the-icon-sign-of-unity-or-division-pt-4/.
———. "The Icon: Sign of Unity or Division?" Pt. 5. *Orthodox Arts Journal*, July 11, 2012. https://www.orthodoxartsjournal.org/the-icon-sign-of-unity-or-division-pt-5/.
———. "The Icon: Sign of Unity or Division?" Pt. 6. *Orthodox Arts Journal*, July 20, 2012. https://www.orthodoxartsjournal.org/the-icon-sign-of-unity-or-division-pt-6-conclusion/.
Cavarnos, Constantine. *Orthodox Iconography*. Belmont, MA: Institute for Byzantine and Modern Greek Studies, 1977.
Cleenewerck, Laurent A. *His Broken Body: Understanding and Healing the Schism between the Roman Catholic and Eastern Orthodox Churches*. Washington, DC: Euclid University Consortium, 2007.
Cormack, Robin. "Art and Iconoclasm." In *Oxford Handbook of Byzantine Studies*, edited by Elizabeth Jeffreys et al., 750–57. New York: Oxford University Press, 2008.
Cummings, D. *The Rudder*. Chicago: Orthodox Christian Educational Society, 1957.
Demacopoulos, George E. "The Extraordinary Historical Significance of Ecumenical Patriarch Bartholomew's Presence at Pope Francis' Installation as Bishop of Rome." https://www.archons.org/-/the-extraordinary-historical-significance-of-his-all-holiness-presence-at-pope-francis-installation-as-bishop-of-rome.
Doolan, Patrick. "CIVA Interviews Patrick Doolan." *CIVA Newsletter* 6.2 (1998) 3–6.

BIBLIOGRAPHY

———. *Recovering the Icon: The Life and Work of Leonid Ouspensky*. Biography by Lydia Ouspensky. Crestwood, NY: St. Vladimir's Seminary Press, 2008.
Dulles, Avery. *Models of the Church*. New York: Doubleday, 2002.
Giakalis, Ambrosios. *Images of the Divine: The Theology of Icons at the Seventh Ecumenical Council*. New York: Brill, 1994.
Gros, Jeffrey, et al. *Introduction to Ecumenism*. New York: Paulist, 1998.
Hart, Aidan. *Techniques of Icon and Wall Painting: Egg Tempera, Fresco, Secco*. Leominster, UK: Gracewing, 2011.
Hopko, Thomas. *Speaking the Truth in Love: Education, Mission, and Witness in Contemporary Orthodoxy*. Crestwood, NY: St. Vladimir's Seminary Press, 2004.
Iconographic Arts Institute. "Certificate in Iconographic Arts." Curriculum booklet, 2017.
John of Damascus. *On the Divine Images: Three Apologies against Those Who Attack the Divine Images*. Crestwood, NY: St. Vladimir's Seminary Press, 2003.
John Paul II. *Ut Unum Sint: On Commitment to Ecumenism*. Boston: Pauline, 1995.
Joint International Commission for Theological Dialogue between the Roman Catholic Church and the Orthodox Church. "Synodality and Primacy during the First Millennium: Towards a Common Understanding in Service to the Unity of the Church." September 21, 2016. https://www.ecupatria.org/synodality-and-primacy-during-the-first-millennium-towards-a-common-understanding-in-service-to-the-unity-of-the-church/.
Kasper, Walter. *A Handbook of Spiritual Ecumenism*. Hyde Park, NY: New City, 2007.
Keough, Shawn. Middle Ages lecture. Mount Angel Seminary. St. Benedict, Oregon. February 2012.
Kordis, George. *Icon as Communion: The Ideals and Compositional Principles of Icon Painting*. Translated by Caroline Makropoulos. Brookline, MA: Holy Cross Orthodox Press, 2010.
Louth, Andrew. "Receptive Ecumenism and Catholic Learning—an Orthodox Perspective." In *Receptive Ecumenism and the Call to Catholic Learning: Exploring a Way for Contemporary Ecumenism*, edited by Paul Murray, 361–72. New York: Oxford University Press, 2008.
McPartlan, Paul. "Catholic Learning and Orthodoxy—the Promise and Challenge of Eucharistic Ecclesiology." In *Receptive Ecumenism and the Call to Catholic Learning: Exploring a Way for Contemporary Ecumenism*, edited by Paul Murray, 160–75. New York: Oxford University Press, 2008.
Murray, Paul D. "Receptive Ecumenism and Catholic Learning—Establishing the Agenda." In *Receptive Ecumenism and the Call to Catholic Learning: Exploring a Way for Contemporary Ecumenism*, edited by Paul Murray, 5–25. New York: Oxford University Press, 2008.
Nichols, Aidan. *The Shape of Catholic Theology*. Collegeville, MN: Liturgical Press, 1991.
O'Gara, Margaret. "Receiving Gifts in Ecumenical Dialogue." In *Receptive Ecumenism and the Call to Catholic Learning: Exploring a Way for Contemporary Ecumenism*, edited by Paul Murray, 26–38. New York: Oxford University Press, 2008.
Ouspensky, Leonid A. *Theology in Color: The Frescoes of the Feasts in the Cathedral of the Three Hierarchs in Paris: On the Occasion of the 20th Anniversary of the Repose of Leonid Ouspensky*. Paris: Eglise Orthodoxe Russe en France, 2007.
———. *The Theology of the Icon*. Vols. 1 and 2. Crestwood, NY: St. Vladimir's Seminary Press, 1992.

BIBLIOGRAPHY

Ouspensky, Leonid, and Vladimir Lossky. *The Meaning of Icons*. Crestwood, NY: St. Vladimir's Seminary Press, 1982.

Pelikan, Jaroslav. "Images of the Invisible." In *The Spirit of Eastern Christendom (600–1700)*, 91–145. Chicago: University of Chicago Press, 1974.

Pontifical Council for Promoting Christian Unity. *Directory for the Application of Principles and Norms of Ecumenism*. Washington, DC: USCCB, 1993.

Sahas, Daniel J. *Icon and Logos: Sources in Eighth-Century Iconoclasm*. Toronto: University of Toronto Press, 1986.

Sendler, Egon. *The Icon: Image of the Invisible; Elements of Theology, Aesthetics, and Technique*. Eugene, OR: Wipf and Stock, 2009.

Sievers, Kathy. "History of the Iconographic Arts Institute." Presentation at the Iconographic Arts Institute, Mount Angel, OR, June 2011.

———. "Ten Elements of the Iconographic Arts Institute." Presentation at the Iconographic Arts Institute, Mount Angel, OR, June 2011.

———. "The Vocation of the Iconographer." Presentation at the Iconographic Arts Institute, Mount Angel, OR, June 2011.

Stephanopoulos, Robert G. "Guidelines for Orthodox Christians in Ecumenical Relations." Published by the Standing Conference of Canonical Orthodox Bishops in America. November 1, 1973. http://www.assemblyofbishops.org/about/scobaresources/ecumenical_guidelines.

Tanner, Norman, ed. "Nicaea II." In *Decrees of the Ecumenical Councils*, 1:131–41. Washington, DC: Georgetown University Press, 1990.

Trubetskoi, Eugene N. *Icons: Theology in Color*. Crestwood, NY: St. Vladimir's Seminary Press, 1973.

Vatican II Council. "Lumen Gentium: Dogmatic Constitution on the Church." 1964. In *The Sixteen Documents of Vatican II*, edited by Marianne Lorraine Trouvé, 617–719. Boston: Pauline, 1999.

———."Unitatis Redintegratio: Decree on Ecumenism." 1964. In *The Sixteen Documents of Vatican II*, edited by Marianne Lorraine Trouvé, 229–58. Boston: Pauline, 1999.

Ware, Timothy. *The Orthodox Church*. New York: Penguin, 1997.

Willebrands, Johannes. "The Impact of Dialogue." *Origins* 14 (1985) 720–24.

Yazykova, Irina. *Hidden and Triumphant: The Underground Struggle to Save Russian Iconography*. Brewster, MA: Paraclete, 2010.

www.ingramcontent.com/pod-product-compliance
Lightning Source LLC
Chambersburg PA
CBHW071510150426
43191CB00009B/1466